M000049559

11/2

# Praying Our Days

For Althea:
Blessings and
Good wishes
+ Frank Griswold

# Praying Our Days

## A Guide
## and
## Companion

### Frank T. Griswold

*Twenty-Fifth Presiding Bishop*
*of the Episcopal Church*

 Morehouse Publishing

Scripture readings are taken from The Revised Standard
Version of the Bible © 1973 and from The New Revised
Standard Version of the Bible © 1989 by the National Council
of the Churches of Christ in the U.S.A. Used by permission.

ISBN: 978-0-8192-2359-3
Printed in Canada

Morehouse Publishing, 4775 Linglestown Road,
Harrisburg, PA 17112
Morehouse Publishing, 445 Fifth Avenue,
New York, NY 10016
Morehouse Publishing is an imprint of
Church Publishing Incorporated.
www.churchpublishing.org

09 10 11 12 13 14     10 9 8 7 6 5 4 3 2

✠ ✠ ✠ ✠ ✠

# Contents

✠ ✠ ✠ ✠ ✠

# Acknowledgments

In the pages of this book are reflected the faithfulness, prayer, and companionship of men and women who, across the years, have shared the scripture of their lives with me. As I considered what to say and include in the various sections of this book, I again and again remembered, with a thankful heart, those fellow seekers and servants of the risen Christ, many of whom no longer walk this earth, but continue to be present in that vast fellowship of love and prayer we call the Communion of Saints.

I am particularly grateful too for the editorial wisdom of Barbara Braver, and for the help and direction of Frank Tedeschi of Church Publishing, Inc.

Frank T. Griswold
Bridgewater, New Hampshire
January 1, 2009
The Holy Name of our Lord Jesus Christ

✠ ✠ ✠ ✠ ✠

# Foreword

Many years ago, on a cold January Sunday, I was presented for confirmation in the stately gothic chapel of St. Paul's School in Concord, New Hampshire. Charles Francis Hall, the Bishop of New Hampshire, placed his hands on my head, and the heads of a number of other boys, and solemnly prayed that we would "daily increase. . .more and more" in the Holy Spirit.

Though at some level I understood that this was an important occasion, I must admit I was in a state of uncertainty about what was happening, or what confirmation might ultimately mean. It never occurred to me as I knelt before Bishop Hall that such a seemingly innocent ritual act would become an unexpected doorway through which I would pass to encounters with other bishops as they laid their hands upon me, ordaining me as a deacon, a priest, and a bishop.

Now it is I who have found myself laying my hands on the heads of those equally unsuspecting, wondering what the Holy Spirit might have in store for them in the days ahead. Over the years I have learned that what may appear to be a prescribed ritual moment can lead far beyond itself. Hands are laid upon your head, and you find yourself in an open space of continual growth and discovery you never imagined or anticipated.

Though the details of my confirmation have faded in these intervening years, I remember that following the service the priest who had prepared me and the other boys presented each of us with a gift. It was a devotional manual: a small blue book containing a collection of prayers. There were prayers for each day, for before and after participating in the eucharist, to aid in preparation for the sacramental rite of reconciliation, and to mark the various moments and occasions that occur in the course of our lives. More out of curiosity than overt devotion I began to use the book. Rather unexpectedly it became a companion and a great help in leading me more deeply into the practice of prayer and participation in the sacramental life of the church.

*Since my confirmation, the Episcopal Church has embraced the principles of the Liturgical Movement, which evolved in Europe at the end of the nineteenth and the beginning of the twentieth century and found their way into Anglicanism, largely through the writings of two English monks: Gabriel Hebert and Gregory Dix. Among those principles were a renewed emphasis on the corporate nature of public worship and on the communal rather than the private and personal nature of the eucharist.*

*The 1979 Book of Common Prayer is very much the consequence of the Liturgical Movement. When we come together to participate in liturgical celebrations, we do so not primarily as individuals but as members of a community, namely the body of Christ into which we enter through the sacrament of baptism. As enriching as it has been to recover a sense of the corporate nature of worship, there is still the need for each of us to deepen our companionship with Christ through our personal practices of prayer.*

*This book is offered to assist contemporary Christians both in deepening their life in the Spirit and in enhancing their participation in the sacramental and liturgical life of the church. Its pages bear the mark of my own formation* within the catholic tradition of Anglicanism and the gifts I have received from it. This tradition places a strong emphasis upon regular prayer and sacramental practice. Its stable pattern is intended to sustain us through life's changes and chances, and to shape and form us for service in Christ's name.

In some ways this little book resembles the devotional manual that was so instrumental in teaching me to pray with the church. In addition to a selection of prayers, I have included reflections on spiritual disciplines and practices that have shaped and formed countless men and women across the years.

It is my hope and my prayer for you that this book will be a guide and companion as you pray your days. May what you find in these pages help to expand and deepen your relationship with the risen Christ, the One who loves you and seeks to draw you ever more fully into his ongoing ministry of reconciliation.

✠ ✠ ✠ ✠ ✠

# I

# Lord, Teach Us to Pray

*In the Gospel of Luke the disciples say to Jesus, "Lord, teach us to pray." Ever since, faithful people – like ourselves – who want to learn to pray, have echoed the plea of the disciples. Sometimes the request has a hint of desperation about it because insecurity about how to pray is not uncommon, afflicting even those whose lives are firmly grounded in an ongoing relationship with God. Our ability to pray can actually be undermined by the fear that we don't know how to pray properly, and by our concerns about the purpose and results of our prayer. We may find ourselves plagued by such questions as: Is God meant to answer? Is it selfish to pray for myself? Doesn't God already know before I pray?*

*Such questions have been asked again and again across the ages as prayer has been variously described and understood.*

— 1 —

This is not surprising; at its heart prayer is a means of encountering the Divine, and such encounters defy easy description.

The Catechism in the Book of Common Prayer describes prayer as "responding to God by thought and by deeds with or without words." It also identifies categories of prayer: adoration, praise, thanksgiving, penitence, oblation (the offering of our life and our labor in union with Christ), intercession (prayer for others), and petition (bringing our own needs before God). As these categories represent aspects of a relationship, they overlap and run together. Our prayer life reflects the various dimensions of our ongoing and ever unfolding relationship with God.

As we struggle to know how we are best to be in that relationship, we can take heart from the eighth chapter of the Letter to the Romans in which St. Paul tells us that we do not know how to pray as we ought, and that the Spirit prays within us "with sighs too deep for words." Paul assures us that prayer is an impulse planted deep within us by God's own Spirit. How liberating it is to realize that prayer, at its deepest and truest, is the activity of the Spirit at work in us rather than something we do on our own.

*Madeleine L'Engle, a writer who was shaped by the Anglican tradition and a life of prayer, bears witness in her poem, "Word," to the interior working of the Spirit who transforms our words into revelatory silence. We turn ourselves to the Word, and all the while the Word, who is the risen Christ, is seeking us and praying within us.*

I, who live by words, am wordless when
I try my words in prayer. All language turns
To silence. Prayer will take my words and then
Reveal their emptiness. The stilled voice learns
To hold its peace, to listen with the heart
To silence that is joy, is adoration.
The self is shattered, all words torn apart
In this strange patterned time of contemplation
That, in time, breaks time, breaks words, breaks me,
And then, in silence, leaves me healed and mended.
I leave, returned to language, for I see
Through words, even when all words are ended.

      I, who live by words, am wordless when
      I turn me to the Word to pray. Amen.

*Madeleine L'Engle*

In Psalm 27 the psalmist addresses God, saying: "You speak in my heart and say, 'Seek my face.'" The psalmist is aware that deep within the Spirit is praying, "Seek my face, seek my face, seek my face." The psalmist then yields to the Spirit and responds, "Your face, Lord, will I seek."

In various ways, sometimes in the form of words that well up from deep within, sometimes in the form of a sense of yearning, awe, gratitude, or compassion, God speaks in our hearts and invites us to respond. Our prayer, then, is our response to God's loving invitation. We are to give ourselves over to what the Spirit is already praying within us, even below the level of our consciousness. It is immensely freeing to know that prayer is always going on, and we are to tap into that reality rather than creating the reality ourselves. In order to do so, we must simply be present to the moment. As a contemporary Benedictine teacher of prayer, Dom John Main, has said, prayer is "an openness to love on every level of our being."

Prayer requires what the French writer Gabriel Marcel describes as "availability." When you are "available" your heart and mind are open to the motions of the Spirit who moves within the depths of your being, and who also meets you through the words and presence of others and the circumstances of your life.

A single word of wisdom on the subject of prayer comes from a great teacher of prayer, Thomas Merton. Shortly before his death, he was asked how to pray. His response was: Pray. His practical advice puts me in mind of those of us who love to read and collect recipes but never quite get to the stove. As we learn to cook by cooking, so too we learn to pray by praying.

Another counsel on prayer I have remembered over the years comes from Dom John Chapman, a wise English Benedictine monk. He says: Pray as you can. Don't pray as you can't. Though this seems obvious enough on the surface, at times in my life I have been tempted to emulate one or another of the saints by trying to make my soul fit their particular pattern of prayer. My success has been dismal! Since prayer is a matter of intimacy and companionship with Christ it is always ordered by the Spirit to correspond to the particular shape of our soul. In short, I am meant to meet God as I am, not as if I were St. John of the Cross or Hildegard of Bingen. And, you are meant to meet God as you are: praying as you can, not as you can't.

Prayer, because it is a living relationship, has its seasons in which patterns that have oriented and sustained us may become dry and seemingly lifeless. At such times there is the temptation to blame ourselves for an insufficiency of fervor or attention. In fact, the Spirit may be revealing to us that it is time to move on to some new or deeper encounter with divine Mystery.

I believe the fundamental question we each need to ask ourselves is this: How is the Spirit, the Spirit of Christ, seeking to pray within me and how can I be faithful to that call to prayer? At times ordered patterns of prayer such as those found in the Daily Office section of the Prayer Book can best serve us. At other times we may find ourselves drawn to less formal and more spontaneous ways of praying.

Because Jesus tells us the Spirit "blows where it wills" we must be prepared for those times when the response to our prayer is not what we expected, and also for those instances when we feel our prayer has not been heard. Sometimes when we pray we ask for "answers," and when no answer seems to be forthcoming we are afraid our prayer has gone unheeded. Rabbi Abraham Joshua Heschel reminds us that the purpose of prayer is not information but communion with the Divine.

*That the fruit of our prayer can catch us by surprise indicates the sovereign freedom of the Spirit. I think God wants us to know that the fruit of prayer is the gift of the Spirit and not the result of our efforts. What God chooses to give us, and when God chooses to give it to us, is up to God, as much as we might want certain graces or gifts in particular circumstances. It is always God's choice to take our prayer and use it in whatever ways God in God's love for us desires. We might pray earnestly for quiet confidence and find ourselves continuing to feel anxious. Yet, later on, at a time when we would normally be fearful, we are filled with an unexpected inner reservoir of peace and courage. We are able to act in ways that are far beyond our own perceived capabilities.*

*I would note here that a distinction is sometimes made between prayer and worship, with the underlying assumption that prayer is something personal and private while worship is in a different category. I prefer to think of personal prayer and corporate prayer — that is, liturgical prayer — as profoundly related, sustaining and enriching one another.*

*Our encounter with God, which is at the heart of prayer, can occur as we pray alone in a quiet corner as well as in the* midst of a liturgy. There are times when the proclamation of scripture, the words of the preacher, the prayers of the people, the exchange of the peace, the receiving of communion draw us beyond ourselves into an encounter with Christ. Our prayer in our quiet corner may have worked in us an increased capacity to recognize Christ's presence in the liturgical assembly. At the same time, our liturgical prayer can inform and deepen our personal prayer outside the liturgy.

All prayer, and indeed the desire to pray, flows from the same divine source and leads us deeper into the mystery we call God, which is also the mystery of who we, in grace and truth, are called to be. And indeed prayer is not simply an activity but also a way of being. Through prayer our consciousness is transformed and conformed to the mind of Christ, and we begin to see and act as Christ in us sees and acts. As Julian of Norwich tells us, prayer "ones" us to God.

✣ ✣ ✣ ✣ ✣

# II
# Pray Without Ceasing
## Patterns of Prayer

*It is very easy for us to be overwhelmed by the demands and urgencies of the day, and to lose sight of the fact that God is present in all that the day contains. God is profoundly present in the mystery of time, as season gives way to season and we are shaped by the daily occurrences of our lives. It is our truest work to collaborate with what the Holy Spirit working within us, day by day, is trying to bring about.*

*For many years I have made an annual pilgrimage to a Benedictine monastery in rural upstate New York. In that familiar place I have marked the various turnings in my life by times of prayer and reflection. The crypt of the monastery chapel is an octagonal space, and as you stand within it you* are surrounded by a series of stained-glass windows. These windows, with their rich and varied hues, symbolically depict the days of the week, the seasons of the year, the hours of the day, and the life span of the monk. Collectively, the windows represent the mystery of time: the beginning and end of life and the hours, days, months, seasons, and years through which we are shaped and formed and drawn into another mystery, which is the mystery of our own identity, and who God knows us and calls us to be. When I visit the monastery I am drawn again and again to this quiet crypt so that I might spend time pondering what has occurred in my life and how – in both hidden and obvious ways – time has left its mark upon me.

We might view the Book of Common Prayer as a celebration of the mystery of time. Through the ordering of its pages time is broken open and made revelatory of the reality of our life in Christ. The Prayer Book's patterns of daily prayer, its weekly cycle of scripture and sacrament, its celebration of the seasons of the Church Year, its marking of the events of our lives, from birth to death, make it a companion as we move through our days as sojourners journeying toward maturity in Christ.

The Church Year with its succession of seasons, festivals, and fasts, allows us to ponder and appropriate what St. Paul calls "the mystery of Christ." The progressive celebration of the life and deeds of Jesus in the seasons of the Church Year allows us to inhabit his life in such a way that it no longer remains external to us but becomes part of who we are.

The Church Year, or Liturgical Year as it is also called, falls into two cycles; the first may be termed Incarnation and the second Redemption. The Incarnation cycle focuses on the mystery of the Word becoming flesh and dwelling among us. The Redemption cycle calls to mind the saving work of that same incarnate Word in the death and resurrection of Jesus and the outpouring of the Holy Spirit upon the disciples.

Each cycle is preceded by a season of preparation. In the first cycle, during the season of Advent, we prepare for the Incarnation as various aspects of Christ's coming are set before us. The twelve days of Christmas, which span the time between Christmas Eve and the Feast of the Epiphany, mark the coming of the Word. Epiphany, together with the Baptism of Jesus, further unfold the mystery of the Incarnation as an act of divine self-disclosure and revelation.

*The second cycle, Redemption, begins with another season of preparation: Lent. The Forty days of Lent lead us to Holy Week and Easter with the solemn commemoration of the death and resurrection of Jesus. Because Christ's resurrection is the determining reality for the life of the church, Easter Day is extended into a season of Fifty days treated as one continuous celebration. The Great Fifty Days, as the Easter season is called, culminate in Pentecost and the celebration of the extension of the resurrection into our lives through the gift of the Holy Spirit.*

*Epiphany and Pentecost are both succeeded by a series of Sundays, sometimes called "ordinary time," in which the Gospels of Matthew, Mark, and Luke are read successively over a period of three years.*

*The celebration of these seasons is accompanied by changes in the decoration of the church, and the employment of various signs and symbols. These signs and symbols are to assist us in entering more deeply into the mystery of Christ conveyed through the seasons of the Church Year.*

# Prayers to Mark the Seasons of the Church Year

## Advent

O Day Spring, splendor of eternal light, Sun of Righteousness; come and enlighten the darkness of our minds. O Key of David, come and open wide the secret places of our hearts that we may receive you who came among us at Bethlehem, and who comes among us daily in the unfolding of our lives, and will come again in glory in the age to come. Amen.

## Christmas

O God, who wonderfully created, and yet more wonderfully restored, the dignity of human nature: Grant that we may share the divine life of him who humbled himself to share our humanity, your Son Jesus Christ our Lord. Amen.

## Epiphany

O God, by the leading of a star, at the waters of the Jordan and in the water made wine you revealed your glory in the face of Jesus, your Beloved Son. Grant that we who have been made your children through baptism may show forth your glory in our lives; through Jesus Christ our Savior. Amen.

## Lent

Grant, O Lord, that by the observance of these days of Lent we may grow in companionship with Christ, and that by sharing his sufferings we may come to know the power of his resurrection; this we pray through Jesus Christ, our Redeemer. Amen.

## Easter

O God of peace, you brought back from the dead our Lord Jesus, the great shepherd of the sheep. Make us, through the power of his risen life at work in us, complete in everything good and well pleasing in your sight; through Jesus Christ our Lord. Amen.

## Pentecost

Eternal God whose power at work in us can do infinitely more than we can ask or imagine: enlighten our hearts and minds by your Holy Spirit and lead us into all truth as it is revealed in Christ — who is the way, the truth and the life, and in whose name we pray. Amen.

The Incarnation
   The Passion
      The Resurrection
         The Ascension
            The Coming of the Spirit
was in order that
Christ might abide in us now,
and that we might abide in Him.

*Eric Symes Abbott*

# Familiar prayers and affirmations

## Invocation of the Holy Trinity

✠ In the Name of the Father, and of the Son, and of the Holy Spirit. Amen.

*✠ indicates places where the Sign of the Cross is traditionally made. See page 158.*

## The Lord's Prayer

*Jesus himself has given us the words of the Lord's Prayer, as we are told in the gospels, and therefore when we pray this prayer we are joining our prayer with the unceasing prayer of the risen Christ.*

Our Father who art in
          heaven,
  hallowed be thy Name,
  thy kingdom come,
  thy will be done,
      on earth as it is in
          heaven.
Give us this day our
          daily bread.
And forgive us our
          trespasses,
  as we forgive those
      who trespass against us.
And lead us not into
          temptation,
  but deliver us from evil.
For thine is the kingdom,
  and the power, and
          the glory,
  for ever and ever.
Amen.

Our Father in heaven,
  hallowed be your
          Name,
  your kingdom come,
  your will be done,
      on earth as in
          heaven.
Give us today our
          daily bread.
Forgive us our sins
  as we forgive those
  who sin against us.
Save us from the time
      of trial,
  and deliver us from
      evil.
For the kingdom,
      the power,
  and the glory are yours,
  now and forever.
Amen.

Eternal Spirit,

Earth-maker, Pain-bearer, Life-giver,

Source of all that is and that shall be,

Father and Mother of us all,

Loving God, in whom is heaven:

The hallowing of your name echo through the universe!

The way of your justice be followed by the peoples
        of the world!

Your heavenly will be done by all created beings!

Your commonwealth of peace and freedom
        sustain our hope and come on earth.

With the bread we need for today, feed us.

In the hurts we absorb from one another, forgive us.

In times of temptation and test, strengthen us.

From trials too great to endure, spare us.

From the grip of all that is evil, free us.

For you reign in the glory of the power that is love,
        now and forever.  Amen.

*A paraphrase of the Lord's Prayer from A New Zealand Prayer Book*

☩

## The Gloria Patri

*This expression of praise, which occurs frequently in the liturgical prayer of the church, can be used at any time as an acknowledgment that we owe our life to the continual sustaining presence of God in God's threefold self-disclosure as Creator, Redeemer, and Sanctifier. It can be said as an act of thanksgiving or renewed focus as the day unfolds.*

Glory to the Father, and to the Son, and to the Holy Spirit: as it was in the beginning, is now, and will be for ever. Amen.

*Another form of the same confession of trinitarian faith is:* Praise to the holy and undivided Trinity, one God: as it was in the beginning, is now, and will be for ever. Amen.

## The Apostles' Creed

*This ancient baptismal confession of faith helps us to recall our own baptism into Christ's death and resurrection whereby we were made limbs of his risen body and sharers in his eternal priesthood.*

I believe in God, the Father almighty,
   creator of heaven and earth.
I believe in Jesus Christ, his only Son our Lord.
   He was conceived by the power of the Holy Spirit
      and born of the Virgin Mary.
   He suffered under Pontius Pilate,
      was crucified, died, and was buried.
   He descended to the dead.
   On the third day he rose again.
   He ascended into heaven,
      and is seated at the right hand of the Father.
   He will come again to judge the living and the dead.
I believe in the Holy Spirit,
   the holy catholic Church,
   the communion of saints,
   the forgiveness of sins,
   the resurrection of the body,
   and the life everlasting.  Amen.

☦

**The Jesus Prayer**

Lord Jesus Christ, Son of the living God, have mercy on me, a sinner.

*This prayer possesses a power all its own. Rooted in the gospels, this brief prayer comes to us from the Eastern Church. A knotted cord is frequently used in conjunction with repetitions of the prayer as an aid to remaining focused while praying. To invoke the name of Jesus is to invoke the risen Christ in the fullness of his all-embracing mercy and love. In this way we invite the Holy Spirit to work in us the mind and heart of Christ. As this occurs our hearts are transfigured and rendered merciful with Christ's own mercy, and we become ever more able to embrace the whole of creation with Christ's own love.*

Lord Jesus Christ, Son of the living God, have mercy on me, a sinner.

## The Hail Mary

*Based upon the words of the angel Gabriel to Mary, recorded in the Gospel of Luke, in this prayer we ask Mary, the theotokos, or "God bearer," the Mother of God, to pray for us.*

Hail Mary, full of grace, the Lord is with you. Blessed are you among women and blessed is the fruit of your womb, Jesus. Holy Mary, Mother of God, pray for us sinners, now, and at the hour of our death. Amen.

## The Angelus

*The Angelus, traditionally recited in the early morning, at noon, and again in the evening, reminds us at the turning points of the day that the Word who became flesh in the "now of this mortal life" is ever present in the most daily and mundane events of our lives. In many churches and monastic communities a bell is rung to announce the Angelus. When prayed in groups, a leader usually introduces each section of the Angelus, as indicated in the italic type, with all joining in for the remainder of each section. When praying by yourself, recite the entire text.*

*The angel of the Lord brought tidings to Mary,*
and she conceived by the Holy Spirit.

Hail Mary, full of grace, the Lord is with you.

Blessed are you among women and blessed is
the fruit of your womb, Jesus.

Holy Mary, Mother of God, pray for us sinners,
now, and at the hour of our death.

*Behold the handmaid of the Lord:* let it be to me
according to your word.

Hail Mary, full of grace, the Lord is with you.

Blessed are you among women and blessed is
the fruit of your womb, Jesus.

Holy Mary, Mother of God, pray for us sinners,
now, and at the hour of our death.

*The word was made flesh*, and dwelt among us.

Hail Mary, full of grace, the Lord is with you.

Blessed are you among women and blessed is the
fruit of your womb, Jesus.

Holy Mary, Mother of God, pray for us sinners,
now, and at the hour of our death.

*Pray for us, O holy Mother of God*, that we may be
made worthy of the promises of Christ.

*Let us pray.*

Pour your grace into our hearts, O Lord, that we who
have known the incarnation of your Son Jesus Christ,
announced by an angel to the Virgin Mary, ✠ may
by his cross and passion be brought to the glory of his
resurrection; who lives and reigns with you, in the unity
of the Holy Spirit, one God, now and for ever. *Amen.*

✠

# Regina Coeli

*From Easter Day until the Day of Pentecost the Regina Coeli is said in place of the Angelus.*

Queen of Heaven, be joyful, Alleluia.

Because he whom you were worthy to bear, Alleluia.

has risen as he promised, Alleluia.

For us, to God, pour forth your prayer, Alleluia.

*Rejoice and be glad, O Virgin Mary, Alleluia.*

For the Lord is risen indeed, Alleluia!

*Let us pray.*

O God, through the resurrection of your Son Jesus Christ you have brought joy into the world: grant that we, aided by the prayers of the Virgin Mary, his Mother, ✠ may be brought to the joys of everlasting life. This we pray through Jesus Christ, our Lord.

*Amen.*

✠

# Brief Centering Prayers

*When Jesus found himself tempted by the Devil in the wilderness he invoked short passages of scripture to offset the words of the tempter. In the early centuries of the Christian church it was common practice to call to mind phrases of scripture to ground oneself in the midst of trials and struggles. The familiar phrases* O God, make speed to save us; O Lord, make haste to help us *— which have found their way into various forms of daily prayer — were invocations commonly used by the Desert Fathers and Mothers of the fourth century.*

*Phrases to which we may be drawn, from scripture or some other source, can help us to be recollected and grounded in the midst of circumstances that might otherwise overwhelm us. Once they become part of us they can be called to mind, or may even emerge on their own, when we most need them.*

*One phrase, for example, that has helped me in difficult moments is from the writings of the French Jesuit, Pierre Teilhard de Chardin:*

By means of all created things, without exception, the Divine assails us, penetrates us, and molds us.

☩

O God, make speed to save me; O Lord, make haste
to help me.

✠

Glory to God whose power working in me can do
infinitely more than I can ask or imagine.

✠

I can do all things through Christ who strengthens me.

✠

Into your hands I commend my spirit.

✠

My grace is sufficient.

✠

Come, Holy Ghost, my soul inspire.

✠

O God, you are my God; eagerly I seek you.

✠

In the time of my trouble I will call upon you.

✠

You are my refuge and my strength.

✠

Create in me a clean heart, O God.

✠

Lord, have mercy; Christ, have mercy; Lord, have mercy.

⊹

# The Daily Office

*Through the centuries it has been the practice of Christians
and others to mark the turnings of the day with prayer. This
practice led to the formation of specific patterns or offices
of prayer to sustain our awareness that in whatever we are
doing God is also present.*

*The Daily Office, as found in the Book of Common Prayer,
is rooted in this ancient tradition. Daily praying of the principal offices of Morning Prayer and Evening Prayer does much
more than mark the beginning and ending of the day. Over
time the repetition of their subtle rhythms can profoundly af-
fect us and form Christ in us. The praying of the psalms and
the reading of God's word help us both to widen our vision
and to situate ourselves and the day at hand within the ever
unfolding mystery of God's larger purposes. The other two
offices, Noonday Prayer and Compline, can also aid us in
forming a daily pattern of attentiveness to God's presence in
the midst of our often busy and hectic lives.*

The following brief forms for daily prayer found in the Prayer Book (Daily Devotions for Individuals and Families) also provide opportunities to mark the turnings of the day. In their structure they represent simplifications of the four offices. I have suggested additional passages of scripture, one for each day of the week, which may be used for reflection and meditation. I have also added some prayers and suggestions for reflection to help you in the midst of the day's demands. The asterisks in the psalms are an invitation to pause for reflection.

## In the Morning

*From Psalm 51*

Open my lips, O Lord, *
   and my mouth shall proclaim your praise.

Create in me a clean heart, O God, *
   and renew a right spirit within me.

Cast me not away from your presence *
   and take not your holy Spirit from me.

Give me the joy of your saving help again *
   and sustain me with your bountiful Spirit.

Glory to the Father, and to the Son, and to the
·          Holy Spirit: *
as it was in the beginning, is now, and will be
          for ever.  Amen.

*A Reading for Sunday*

Blessed be the God and Father of our Lord Jesus
Christ! By his great mercy we have been born anew to
a living hope through the resurrection of Jesus Christ
from the dead.   *1 Peter 1:3*

*A Reading for Monday*

The word is near you; it is in your mouth and in your
heart for you to observe.   *Deuteronomy 30:14*

*A Reading for Tuesday*

Though the Lord may give you the bread of adversity
and the water of affliction, yet your Teacher will not
hide himself any more, but your eyes shall see your
Teacher. And when you turn to the right or when you
turn to the left, your ears shall hear a word behind you,
saying, "This is the way; walk in it."   *Isaiah 30:20-21*

## A Reading for Wednesday

To him who loves us and freed us from our sins by his blood, and made us to be a kingdom, priests serving his God and Father, to him be glory and dominion for ever and ever. Amen. *Revelation 1:5-6*

## A Reading for Thursday

Jesus said: "I am the bread of life. Whoever comes to me will never be hungry and whoever believes in me will never be thirsty." *John 6:35*

## A Reading for Friday

Jesus said: "My food is to do the will of him who sent me and to complete his work. . . And I, when I am lifted up from the earth, will draw all people to myself." *John 4:34; 12:32*

## A Reading for Saturday

God saw everything that he had made, and indeed it was very good. . . And on the seventh day God finished the work that he had done and he rested from all the work that he had done. *Genesis 1:31; 2:2*

*Prayers may be added for yourself and others. Here are some suggestions.*
*See pages 51-53 for suggested daily intentions.*

My heart is firmly fixed, O God, my heart is fixed;

I will sing and make melody.

Wake up, my spirit;

awake, lute and harp;

I myself will waken the dawn.   *Psalm 108*

☩

## A Morning Offering

Lord, grant me to greet the coming day in peace.

Help me to rely upon your holy will.

In every hour of the day reveal your will to me.

Bless my dealings with all who surround me.

Teach me to treat all that comes to me throughout

the day with peace of soul

and with firm belief that your will governs all.

Guide my words and deeds, my thoughts and feelings.

Teach me to act firmly and wisely, without

embittering or embarrassing others.

Give me strength to bear the fatigue of the coming

day with all that it shall bring.

Direct my will, teach me to pray, pray yourself in me.
    Amen.

*Philaret, Metropolitan of Moscow, 1821-1867*

Be present with me, O Christ, in all the events and
    encounters of this day.
Bless those who will cross my path,
And be with me especially as I [.......].
Grant that all I say and do may flow from your Spirit
    who prays within me.
Keep me safe from all dangers, and in moments of
    frustration or failure let me not despair
    of your ever-present mercy and enfolding love.

May blessed Mary, [ _____,] and all the saints support
and uphold me with their companionship and their
prayers, and may all that I do and say this day be to
your praise and glory.

Almighty and eternal God,

so draw my heart to you,

so guide my mind,

so fill my imagination,

so control my will,

that I may be wholly yours,

utterly dedicated to you,

and then use me,

I pray,

and always to your glory

and for the welfare of your people.

I ask this in the name of our Savior, Jesus Christ.

Amen.

*Adapted from the Prayer Book*

*Thanksgiving for Baptism*

Blessed are you, holy and living God. Through baptism you have made me a living member of Christ's risen body and called me to share his eternal priesthood. May your Spirit continue to form Christ in me and make me, in word and example, a minister of his reconciling love. This I pray in the name of the One in whom you have reconciled all things to yourself. Amen.

*The Lord's Prayer*

*The Collect*

Lord God, almighty and everlasting Father, you have brought us in safety to this new day: Preserve us with your mighty power, that we may not fall into sin, nor be overcome by adversity; and in all we do, direct us to the fulfilling of your purpose; through Jesus Christ our Lord. Amen.

✠ Glory to God whose power, working in us, can do infinitely more than we can ask or imagine: Glory to him from generation to generation in the Church, and in Christ Jesus for ever and ever. Amen.

*Ephesians 3:20, 21*

## At Noon

*From Psalm 113*

Give praise, you servants of the LORD; *
    praise the Name of the LORD.
Let the Name of the LORD be blessed, *
    from this time forth for evermore.
From the rising of the sun to its going down *
    let the Name of the LORD be praised.
The LORD is high above all nations, *
    and his glory above the heavens.

*A Reading*

O God, you will keep in perfect peace those whose minds are fixed on you; for in returning and rest we shall be saved; in quietness and trust shall be our strength.

*Isaiah 26:3; 30:15*

*Prayers may be offered for ourselves and others. See pages 51-53 for suggested daily intentions.*

*The Lord's Prayer*

*The Collect*

Blessed Savior, at this hour you hung upon the cross, stretching out your loving arms: Grant that all the peoples of the earth may look to you and be saved; for your mercies' sake. Amen.

*or this*

Lord Jesus Christ, you said to your apostles, "Peace I give to you; my own peace I leave with you:" Regard not our sins, but the faith of your Church, and give to us the peace and unity of that heavenly City, where with the Father and the Holy Spirit you live and reign, now and for ever. Amen.

✠ May the God of hope fill us with all joy and peace in believing through the power of the Holy Spirit. Amen. *Romans 15:13*

## In the Early Evening

### REFLECTION AND REVIEW AT THE END OF THE DAY

*It is a helpful practice to take a few minutes in the evening to reflect upon the events and encounters of the past day. Our days are filled with "letters from God," the poet Walt Whitman tells us. However, we seldom take the time to read* them. Ask the Holy Spirit to help you read your letters from God. Ask what the blessings, and the burdens, of the day have been. What invitations and insights have been revealed? How has Christ been present in the midst of all that has happened as companion and teacher? Do not strain for answers to these questions. Simply let the Holy Spirit move freely within you. As you begin you might wish to pray the following prayer, which is based upon a portion of Psalm 139.

Lord, you have searched me out and known me;
    you know my sitting down and my rising up;
    you discern my thoughts from afar.
You trace my journeys and my resting places
    and are acquainted with all my ways.

Be with me in this evening hour
    and bring to my awareness how you have been
    present this day: in those I have encountered
    and in all that has occurred.

If there are things for which you feel the need for forgiveness, you might offer them to God in the context of the Lord's Prayer or in conjunction with the Jesus Prayer. As you do so remember the words of St. Benedict: "Never despair of God's mercy." For as we are told in the psalms, "the Lord is full of compassion and mercy."

*End your time of recollection by giving God thanks for the gifts and graces of the day as well as for those things that have been challenging or difficult. You might conclude your thanksgiving with the Gloria Patri. Then pray this evening hymn:*

O Gracious Light,
pure brightness of the everliving Father in heaven,
O Jesus Christ, holy and blessed!

Now as we come to the setting of the sun,
and our eyes behold the vesper light,
we sing your praises, O God: Father, Son, and Holy
    Spirit.

You are worthy at all times to be praised by happy
    voices,
O Son of God, O Giver of life,
and to be gloried through all the worlds.

### A Reading for Sunday

It is not ourselves that we proclaim; we proclaim Christ Jesus as Lord, and ourselves as your servants, for Jesus' sake. For the same God who said, "Out of darkness let light shine," has caused his light to shine within us, to give the light of revelation—the revelation of the glory of God in the face of Jesus Christ.   *2 Corinthians 4:5-6*

### A Reading for Monday

If anyone is in Christ, there is a new creation: everything old has passed away; see, everything has become new! All this is from God, who reconciled us to himself through Christ, and has given us the ministry of reconciliation; that is, in Christ God was reconciling the world to himself.   *2 Corinthians 5:17-19*

### A Reading for Tuesday

Jesus said, "Come to me all you that are weary and are carrying heavy burdens, and I will give you rest. Take my yoke upon you, and learn from me; for I am gentle and humble in heart, and you will find rest for your souls. For my yoke is easy, and my burden is light."   *Matthew 11:28-30*

*A Reading for Wednesday*

I pray that, according to the riches of God's glory, he may grant that you may be strengthened in your inner being with power through his Spirit, and that Christ may dwell in your hearts through faith, as you are being rooted and grounded in love. I pray that you may have the power to comprehend, with all the saints, what is the breadth and length and height and depth, and to know the love of Christ that surpasses knowledge, so that you may be filled with all the fullness of God. *Ephesians 3:16-19*

*A Reading for Thursday*

Suffering produces endurance, and endurance produces character, and character produces hope, and hope does not disappoint us, because God's love has been poured into our hearts through the Holy Spirit that has been given to us. *Romans 5:3-5*

*A Reading for Friday*

Whoever does not take up the cross and follow me is not worthy of me. Those who find their life will lose it, and those who lose their life for my sake will find it. *Matthew 10:38*

*A Reading for Saturday*

As you therefore have received Christ Jesus the Lord, continue to live your lives in him rooted and built up in him and established in the faith, just as you were taught, abounding in thanksgiving. *Colossians 2:6-7*

*Prayers may be added for yourself and others. See pages 51-53 for suggested daily intentions.*

*The Lord's Prayer*

*The Collect*

Lord Jesus, stay with us, for evening is at hand and the day is past; be our companion in the way, kindle our hearts, and awaken hope, that we may know you as you are revealed in Scripture and the breaking of bread. Grant this for the sake of your love. Amen.


✠ The grace of our Lord Jesus Christ, and the love of God, and the fellowship of the Holy Spirit be with us all evermore. Amen. *2 Corinthians 13:14*

## At the Close of Day

*Psalm 134*

Behold now, bless the LORD, all you servants of
      the LORD, *

   you that stand by night in the house of the LORD.

Lift up your hands in the holy place and bless
      the LORD; *

   the LORD who made heaven and earth bless you
      out of Zion.

*A Reading*

Lord, you are in the midst of us and we are called
by your Name: Do not forsake us, O Lord our God.

*Jeremiah 14:9, 22*

*The following may be said*

Lord, you now have set your servant free *

   to go in peace as you have promised;

For these eyes of mine have seen the Savior, *

   whom you have prepared for all the world to see:

A Light to enlighten the nations, *

   and the glory of your people Israel.

*Prayers for yourself and others may follow. It is appropriate that prayers of thanksgiving for the blessings of the day, and penitence for sins, be included. See pages 51-53 for suggested daily intentions.*

## As You Prepare for Sleep

Guide me waking, O Lord, and guard me sleeping; that awake I may watch with Christ, and asleep I may rest in peace. Amen.

☩

Lord
it is night.
The night is for stillness.
    Let us be still in the presence of God.

It is night after a long day.
    What has been done has been done;
    what has not been done has not been done;
    let it be.

The night is dark.
    Let our fears of the darkness of the world and
        of our own lives
    rest in you.

The night is quiet.

> Let the quietness of your peace enfold us,
>> all dear to us,
>> and all who have no peace.

The night heralds the dawn.

> Let us look expectantly to a new day,
>> new joys,
>> new possibilities.

In your name we pray.
Amen.

*A New Zealand Prayer Book*

*The Lord's Prayer*

*The Collect*
Visit this place, O Lord, and drive far from it all snares of the enemy; let your holy angels dwell with us to preserve us in peace; and let your blessing be upon us always; through Jesus Christ our Lord. Amen.

✠ The almighty and merciful Lord, Father, Son, and Holy Spirit, bless us and keep us. Amen.

꙳

# Prayer Before Meals

*Before beginning a meal we remember that all we have is God's gift, including the food before us. This is also a moment to call to mind those who go hungry. The sign of the cross may accompany the prayer.*

Bless, O Lord, these gifts which through your goodness, and the work of human hands, we are about to receive. As this food strengthens and sustains us, may we strengthen and sustain others out of the riches of your grace. This we pray through Jesus Christ Our Lord.

*The Book of Common Prayer includes these brief prayers to say at mealtime.*

Give us grateful hearts, our Father, for all your mercies, and make us mindful of the needs of others; through Jesus Christ our Lord. Amen.

Bless, O Lord, your gifts to our use and us to your service; for Christ's sake. Amen.

Blessed are you, O Lord God, King of the Universe, for you give us food to sustain our lives and make our hearts glad; through Jesus Christ our Lord. Amen.

For these and all his mercies, God's holy Name be blessed and praised; through Jesus Christ our Lord. Amen.

## Prayer After Meals

May the food we have received strengthen us for service. In the name of the Father and of the Son and of the Holy Spirit. Amen.

May Christ, the Lord of glory, make us partakers of the banquet of unending life. Amen.

# Praying for Others

*Prayer is a form of energy. It is a manifestation of the Holy Spirit, who is the minister of communion. The Holy Spirit is the source of unity between the Father and the Son and between us and the Father and the Son and all living things. To pray for others is to acknowledge and call upon this energy whose dominant characteristic is love, a love which exceeds all we might ask or imagine, a love which transcends boundaries of life and death, of sickness and health, a love that can endure all things and hope all things.*

*The consequence of praying for others lies in God's hands and is beyond our knowing. But this we do know: no energy of the Spirit is ever wasted, even though our limited vision may make it impossible to see the fruit of the Spirit's activity.*

*The Spirit's movements within us do not always take the form of words and therefore to think of another and to desire their well-being is in itself prayer. As well, the Spirit can move us to some form of action on behalf of another. Such actions are also a form of prayer.*

*A prayer composed by St. Augustine of Hippo, which is included in the Office of Evening Prayer in the Book of*

Common Prayer, captures many aspects of our care and concern for others. As you say this prayer, you might call to mind particular persons.

Keep watch, dear Lord, with those who work, or watch, or weep this night, and give your angels charge over those who sleep. Tend the sick, Lord Christ; give rest to the weary, bless the dying, soothe the suffering, pity the afflicted, shield the joyous; and all for your love's sake. Amen.

*When we pray for someone close to us who is ill, our deepest desire is that they be restored to health. Our earnest longing and deep loving for the other may well result in a restoration of health. Jesus in the gospels performed many healings, and healing is a continuing work of the risen Christ. This we know: our prayers will be received and honored and we can offer them in a spirit of expectant trust.*

*We also know that the love and concern at the heart of our prayer will not be wasted, though how God will use our prayer exceeds our limited knowing. Prayer may produce peace or quiet confidence in those for whom we pray. Prayer may give us an increased capacity to companion them in what they are living or suffering. Our prayer may lead to immediate and tangible support they need in order to bear their present burdens.*

⁙

*The following prayer, adapted from a prayer originating in the Indian Subcontinent, is animated by an awareness of the energy that comes from God's boundless love flowing as a stream, through us, and through the one for whom we pray and returning to God.*

Jesus, let your healing love which flows from your
      cross
flow through your Spirit into my spirit and into
      _____'s spirit.
Heal _____ and let your healing love flow into the
      depths of _____'s heart and mind.
Let healing love find its way into all parts of _____'s
      body
      bringing with it wholeness, health and peace.

Let healing love flow back to my spirit, and back to
        you, so that a stream of healing love
flowing from you, through me, and through
        _____ and returning to you
may make _____ whole,
and may make me whole.
Glory to you, and praise and thanksgiving now
        and forever.
Amen.


*Because those closest to us and their needs naturally take
precedence in our prayer for others, we may need to ask the
Holy Spirit, who teaches us to pray, to help us to extend
the embrace of our prayer to include the needs of the world
in which we live and move and have our being. The daily
news provides many invitations to be stretched by the Spirit
to pray for those both far and near, and for the wellbeing of
"this fragile earth" we call our home. In addition, the following list of intentions for the days of the week may help you
expand the range of your prayer:*

## Sunday

The universal church, its unity in witness and
mission

My local congregation and all who worship with me

Bishops and all others who hold positions of
leadership in the church

The leaders of the nations and those who hold
public office

The natural world and its resources

## Monday

Those engaged in the media and the arts

Those engaged in farming and fishing

Those engaged in commerce and industry

Those engaged in finance and service

Those whose work is dangerous, stressful, or
unrewarding

All who are unemployed or under-employed

## Tuesday

All who are sick in mind, body, or spirit

Those in the midst of famine or disaster

Victims of abuse and violence, prejudice, or hatred

Those suffering grief or loss

Those engaged is the medical and healing
    professions


## Wednesday

Those who deliver social services and their clients

All who work in the criminal justice system

Victims of crime and for the perpetrators

Aid agencies and their work throughout the world

Those living in poverty or under oppression


## Thursday

Local government and community leaders

Those who provide local services

Emergency and rescue organizations

Those who work with young or elderly people

Schools, colleges, and universities

## Friday

The President, members of Congress, and the armed
   forces

Justice and peace in the world

An equitable distribution of the world's resources

Those who work for reconciliation among peoples
   and nations

Those whose lives are devastated by war, civil strife,
   or natural disasters

Prisoners, refugees, immigrants, the homeless and
   forgotten


## Saturday

Our households, families, friends, and all whom we love

Those whose time is spent caring for others

Those with terminal illnesses or close to death

Those who have died

The communion of saints

*After the Church of England Book of Daily Prayer*

✠ ✠ ✠ ✠ ✠

# III

# I Have Met You in Your Sacraments

*Encounters with Christ*

St. Ambrose of Milan, speaking of the sacraments, exclaimed: "You have shown yourself to me, O Christ, face to face. I have met you in your sacraments." Christ is present in the proclamation and preaching of the word, in the community gathered for worship, and in the sacramental signs of bread and wine by which we are nourished and fed. Indeed, Christ is truly present in all the sacramental rites and, through an array of signs and symbols, words and gestures, continues to meet us, heal us, and empower us for service.

The Catechism in the Book of Common Prayer tells us that the two great sacraments given by Christ to his church are Holy Baptism and the Holy Eucharist, and that other sacramental rites which evolved in the life of the church include confirmation, ordination, holy matrimony, reconciliation of a penitent, and the laying on of hands and anointing of the sick. Included in the Prayer Book are liturgical forms for the celebration of each of these sacramental rites.

Holy Baptism gives us our identity as members of Christ's risen body, while the Holy Eucharist strengthens and deepens that identity as we grow into the fullness of being, which is described by St. Paul as "growing up in all ways into Christ." Along the way we stumble again and again and dishonor our baptismal identity through our sinfulness. The rite of reconciliation provides a way to return home to God's mercy and to be restored to companionship with Christ and the other members of his body. In the following sections we will seek to enter more deeply into the encounter with the risen Christ provided by the sacramental rites of Holy Baptism, Holy Eucharist, and the Reconciliation of a Penitent.

# Holy Baptism

*In baptism we are made one with Christ. Christ's risen life is declared at work in us through the action of the Holy Spirit. The life we now live is no longer our own but, as St. Paul tells us, it is Christ who lives in us. Paul also says that in baptism we are buried with Christ in his death in order to rise with Christ to newness of life. Baptism, therefore, unites us to Christ in an ongoing dynamic of dying and rising. Our realization that we have been drawn into the dying and rising of Christ – the "paschal mystery" – helps us to make sense of the various dyings and risings, some large and some small, that we experience throughout our lives.*

*In baptism we also celebrate the fact that our lives are woven together with the lives of others in a vast web of relationships which St. Paul calls the body of Christ. As such, we are the limbs of that body through which Christ, over the centuries and in our own day, continues his work of healing and reconciling and making all things new.*

*As limbs of Christ's body, we live lives of communion. Communion, however, is more than a matter of human relationships. Communion has to do with the inner life of God as lived by the three Persons of the Holy Trinity. This life of* communion is an outpouring of love: the love between the Father and the Son in the Holy Spirit. We might visualize the relationship of the Trinity as an eternal circle dance of the Father, the Son, and the Holy Spirit: a circle dance of love.

Through baptism we are taken into that circle dance. The Holy Spirit, the minister of communion, pours the love of God into our hearts and gives us the ability to respond to God's love with our own answering love. Our answering love is the Spirit of Christ loving the Father and the whole creation in and through us.

Because many of us were baptized as infants, the memory of this transformative event is lost from our consciousness. Thus, when we reflect upon our baptism we do so largely in terms of the Baptismal Covenant set out in the Book of Common Prayer, which calls us to a life of proclamation, witness, and service. We tend to overlook the fact that at its heart baptism is about our relationship to Christ. It is not primarily about what we are called to do but more fundamentally about our identity: who we have been made by water and the Holy Spirit.

Baptism is a mystery. That is, through the pouring of water and the invocation of the Holy Trinity a reality larger than anything we can easily comprehend envelopes us and we spend a lifetime appropriating its meaning and consequences. Living this mystery invites us to ponder and reflect upon what it means to be united with Christ.

## A Prayer of Thanksgiving for My Baptism

Gracious God, through the waters of baptism and the working of the Holy Spirit, you have made me one with Christ in his death and resurrection. I have become a limb and member of Christ's risen body, the Church. You have sealed and marked me by the Holy Spirit as Christ's own forever and called me to share in his eternal priesthood. Sustain and strengthen me with your Spirit day by day. Give me an inquiring and discerning heart, the courage to will and to persevere, a spirit to know and to love you, and the gift of joy and wonder in all your works. In the face of difficulty and distress help me to remember that my life is not my own but the life that Christ lives in me, and that your power working in me can do infinitely more than I can ask or imagine. To you be glory in the Church and in Christ Jesus, now and forever. Amen.

﹢

*The Baptismal Covenant invites our prayerful reflection as a way of regrounding ourselves in our baptismal identity and all that is therefore required of us. The first five questions have to do with the mystery of God's self-disclosure as Father, Son, and Holy Spirit and our relationship to that mystery through our participation in the body of Christ. The fifth question is a call to self-examination and an acknowledgment that evil is a reality, and that our sinfulness requires our awareness and repentance. The last three questions concern our willingness to live lives of proclamation, witness, and service, empowered by our life in Christ in all its fullness.*

## The Baptismal Covenant

*Celebrant* Do you believe in God the Father?

*People*    I believe in God, the Father almighty,
creator of heaven and earth.


*Celebrant* Do you believe in Jesus Christ,
the Son of God?

*People*    I believe in Jesus Christ, his only Son,
our Lord.

He was conceived by the power of the Holy
Spirit and born of the Virgin Mary.

He suffered under Pontius Pilate,
was crucified, died, and was buried.

He descended to the dead.

On the third day he rose again.

He ascended into heaven,
and is seated at the right hand of
the Father.

He will come again to judge the living
and the dead.

*Celebrant* Do you believe in God the Holy Spirit?

*People*    I believe in the Holy Spirit,

the holy catholic Church,

the communion of saints,

the forgiveness of sins,

the resurrection of the body,

and the life everlasting.

*Celebrant* Will you continue in the apostles' teaching

and fellowship, in the breaking of bread,

and in the prayers?

*People*    I will, with God's help.

*Celebrant* Will you persevere in resisting evil, and,

whenever you fall into sin, repent and

return to the Lord?

*People*    I will, with God's help.

*Celebrant* Will you proclaim by word and example

the Good News of God in Christ?

*People*    I will, with God's help.

*Celebrant* Will you seek and serve Christ in all
persons, loving your neighbor as yourself?

*People* I will, with God's help.

*Celebrant* Will you strive for justice and peace among
all people, and respect the dignity of every
human being?

*People* I will, with God's help.

Almighty God,

in the paschal mystery of Jesus' death and
resurrection

you established the new covenant of reconciliation.

Grant that I, and all who have been reborn into the
fellowship of Christ's body,

may show forth in our lives

what we profess as our faith.

This I pray through Jesus Christ our Lord.

Amen.

*Adapted from the Book of Common Prayer*

# The Holy Eucharist

*The Holy Eucharist is, as the Book of Common Prayer declares,
"the principal act of Christian worship on the Lord's Day." The
eucharist is also frequently celebrated on weekdays, Holy Days, at
particular moments in the course of our lives – such as weddings
and funerals – and at various moments in the life of the church.
This has not always been the case. Within my memory it was
common for the eucharist to be celebrated as the principal Sunday
service only once a month. Its infrequency served to heighten the
sense of the eucharist as an extraordinary gift. Given its present
frequent celebration, there is the danger that it can be approached
with a casual spirit as if it were routine and commonplace.*

*At its heart the eucharist is an encounter with the risen Christ.
Mindfulness of what we are doing when we come together to
celebrate the eucharist prepares us to recognize Christ coming
to us in word and sacrament and in the community gathered
for worship. The eucharistic elements are the means whereby a
dynamic and ongoing process of growing up into Christ takes
place in us. As the limbs of Christ's risen body, bound together
in baptism, we are collectively brought to maturity.*

*I am grateful for the devotional books with their prayers of
preparation and thanksgiving that played an important role in*

*shaping my eucharistic consciousness. It is my hope that the fol-*
*lowing prayers will help you to enlarge your awareness of what*
*we are about when we come together to celebrate the eucharist.*
*May they help you to increase your readiness to receive Christ*
*who seeks to meet you in the course of the liturgy such that you*
*will be sent forth strengthened and renewed to "proclaim by*
*word and example the Good News of God in Christ."*

## Before the Liturgy

Be present in our midst, risen and living Christ. Be
known to us in the scripture we are about to hear, in
our fellowship with one another, and in the breaking
of the bread. Amen.

☩

Give me grace, O Christ, to receive the sacrament of
your Body and Blood, that it may cleanse me of all sin
and nourish me in faith, hope, and love, and all the
fruit of the Spirit. May I be such an ingrafted member
of your Body that your risen life and deathless love
show forth in all that I am, in all that I do, in all that
I say. Amen.

*After William Laud*

With all who have ever sought you,
With all who have ever found you,
With all faithful people in the Body of Christ,
I come to you, O God.
Out of my doubts and fears, I come to acknowledge you.
Out of my forgetfulness, I come to remember you.
Out of my indifference, I come to love you.
Out of my pride, I come with humility.
Out of my sin, I come with repentance.
Out of my discouragement, I come with trust.
Out of my darkness, I come to your light.
Out of my weakness, I come to your strength.
Out of my restlessness, I come to your peace.

M. L. Yates

✠

O God, reunite me with your love by uniting me
    anew with Jesus in these Holy Mysteries.

O God, remind me of your will by the word of
    Christ.

O God, receive my worship in the Perfect Offering
    of Christ.

O God, refresh my soul with the precious Gifts of
    Christ.

O God, recall me to service by the voice of Christ.

*M.L. Yates*

☩

All loving God, just as I am, and with all that I am, I
    come to meet Christ in this eucharist.

I come sick in spirit to the doctor of my soul;

sinful and soiled to the fountain of mercy;

blind to the world's true light;

poor and needy to the One in whom you have
    revealed the riches of your grace.

Heal me, cleanse me, enlighten me.

Enrich my poverty and clothe me in the bright
    garment of your righteousness.

This I pray in the name of Jesus Christ, the true
    bread who gives life to the world.
Amen.

*After St. Thomas Aquinas*

✠

## After Receiving Communion

*Anima Christi*

Soul of Christ, sanctify me;

Body of Christ, save me;

Blood of Christ, refresh me;

Water from the side of Christ, wash me;

Passion of Christ, strengthen me;

O good Jesu, hear me;

Within thy wounds hide me;

Suffer me not to be separated from thee;

From the malicious enemy defend me;

In the hour of my death call me;

And bid me come to thee;

That with thy saints I may praise thee
            forever and ever. Amen.

*XIV Century*

Savior of the world,
our living bread, we have received you outwardly;
let your risen life dwell within us inwardly.
In your strength and courage may we go forth with
   gladness
      to meet you in all life sets before us,
      to seek and serve you in all persons,
      loving our neighbors as ourselves.  Amen.

*After a Nestorian Prayer*

Glory to you, Jesus, my Lord and my God, for feeding my soul with your Body and Blood. Let this heavenly food infuse new life and new vigor into my soul and into the souls of all who have shared this eucharist: that our faith may increase, that we may grow more humble and contrite for our sins, that we may love you and serve you and delight in you and praise you more and more.  Amen.

*After Thomas Ken, 1711*

Lord Jesus Christ, let your sacred Body preserve me to eternal life, and your precious Blood be for the remission of my sins; let the gift and grace of this eucharist be a source of joy and gladness, strength and confidence, that in all I do and say you may be present in the power of your reconciling and healing love. Amen.

*Psalm 150*

*Antiphon:* God gave them grain from heaven:
        so mortals ate the bread of angels.
Hallelujah!
Praise God in his holy temple; *
    praise him in the firmament of his power.
Praise him for his mighty acts; *
    praise him for his excellent greatness.
Praise him with the blast of the ram's-horn; *
    praise him with lyre and harp.
Praise him with timbrel and dance; *
    praise him with strings and pipe.
Praise him with resounding cymbals; *
    praise him with loud-clanging cymbals.

Let everything that has breath *

praise the LORD.

Hallelujah!

*Antiphon:* God gave them grain from heaven:

so mortals ate the bread of angels.

☩

God our Father, whose Son our Lord Jesus Christ in a wonderful Sacrament has left us a memorial of his passion: Grant us so to venerate the sacred mysteries of his Body and Blood, that we may ever perceive within ourselves the fruit of his redemption; who lives and reigns with you and the Holy Spirit, one God, for ever and ever. Amen.

☩

## In the Presence of the Blessed Sacrament: Meditating on the Mystery of the Eucharist

*In many churches and chapels the consecrated elements are set apart after the eucharist for the communion of the sick and others who are unable to be present for the liturgy. A cupboard called an aumbry or tabernacle is used to "reserve" the* sacrament and a lamp burning before the place of reservation indicates the presence of Christ in the eucharistic elements.

Prayer before the Blessed Sacrament can be a way of deepening our appreciation of the eucharist and increasing our wonder that Jesus chose such ordinary signs of nourishment and festivity – bread and wine – to convey his intimate presence to men and women across the ages. The following prayer and meditations are offered for use in the presence of the Blessed Sacrament and also as a way of reflecting on the mystery of the eucharist at other times.

O Thou, Who didst manifest Thyself in the breaking of bread to Thy disciples at Emmaus, grant us ever through the same Blessed Sacrament of thy Presence to know Thee, and love Thee more and more with all our hearts. Abide with us, abide in us, that we may ever abide in Thee; dwell in us that we may ever dwell in Thee, O good Jesu, Thou God of our salvation. Amen.

*Edward Bouverie Pusey*

⟊

When we drink the cup at the eucharist, in which wine has become Christ's blood, his blood mixes with our blood, and they become one. Equally when we eat the bread, which has become the body of Christ, his body mixes with our body, and they become one. This is how, week by week, we are redeemed from sin. . . And in this process, we become part of Christ's body and blood, unified one with another in him. . . Thus in sharing Christ's body and blood, made from bread and wine which are fruits of the earth, we are brought into harmony with the whole of God's creation. In that simple act of receiving the eucharist, we participate in reconciling God with his world.

*St. Irenaeus*

⟊

*These excerpts from "The Holy Communion" by the Angli-
can priest-poet George Herbert (1593-1633) are a profound
meditation on the nature of the eucharist. The poem bears
witness to the hidden and intimate way in which Christ in
the "small quantities" of bread and wine unlocks the secret
places within us — "the soul's most subtle rooms" — which
stand in need of acknowledgment, healing, and integration
into our true self, which is being formed by grace.*

The Holy Communion

Not in rich furniture, or fine array.
    Nor in a wedge of gold,
    Thou, who from me wast sold,
To me dost now thyself convey. . .
. . .by way of nourishment and strength
       Thou creep'st into my breast;
       Making thy way my rest
And thy small quantities my length. . .
Only thy grace, which with these elements comes,
       Knowth the ready way,
       And hath the privy key,
Op'ning the soul's most subtle rooms. . . .

# The Reconciliation of a Penitent

The sacramental rite of the reconciliation of a penitent is a celebration of God's mercy and compassion. When we realize, with the prodigal son in the gospel, that we "have wandered far in a land that is waste," God is always ready to embrace us and welcome us home. Therefore, no matter how burdened or ashamed we may feel because of our sinfulness, the confession of our sins to God in the presence of a priest is a joyful occasion.

While a corporate confession of sin is a regular part of our liturgy, the Prayer Book acknowledges that there may be times when the burden of our sinfulness is so heavy we are unable to quiet our conscience and feel as if we are beyond the reach of God's forgiveness. In such instances, we are urged to seek help and counsel from a "discreet and understanding priest" in whose presence we can confess our sins and receive "the benefit of absolution, and spiritual counsel and advice," laying to rest any scruple and doubt we have about God's desire to reconcile and to forgive.

Some make regular use of this rite as part of their spiritual discipline at such times as Advent and Lent and before Christmas and Easter. Some make their confession only occasionally, while for others the corporate expressions of penitence in the liturgy fulfill their need to confess their sinfulness and be assured of God's pardon. The Anglican tradition regarding making one's confession in the presence of a priest is summed up as follows: "All may, none must, some should."

The rite can take the form of a conversation between priest and penitent or be celebrated more formally. The Book of Common Prayer provides two forms for making one's confession, the shorter of which is included below. In either instance what has been confessed is not normally a matter for subsequent discussion between priest and penitent. Most important, the bond of secrecy of a confession is morally absolute for the priest who receives the confession and must under no circumstances be broken.

*The Penitent begins*

Bless me, for I have sinned.

*The Priest says*

The Lord be in your heart and upon your lips that you may truly and humbly confess your sins: In the Name of the Father, and of the Son, and of the Holy Spirit. *Amen.*

*Penitent*

I confess to Almighty God, to his Church, and to you, that I have sinned by my own fault in thought, word, and deed, in things done and left undone; especially _____. For these and all other sins which I cannot now remember, I am truly sorry. I pray God to have mercy on me. I firmly intend amendment of life, and I humbly beg forgiveness of God and his Church, and ask you for counsel, direction, and absolution.

*Here the Priest may offer counsel, direction, and comfort.*

*The Priest then pronounces this absolution*

Our Lord Jesus Christ, who has left power to his Church to absolve all sinners who truly repent and believe in him, of his great mercy forgive you all your offenses; and by his authority committed to me, I absolve you from all your sins: In the Name of the Father, and of the Son, and of the Holy Spirit. *Amen.*

*or this*

Our Lord Jesus Christ, who offered himself to be sacrificed for us to the Father, and who conferred power on his Church to forgive sins, absolve you through my ministry by the grace of the Holy Spirit, and restore you in the perfect peace of the Church. *Amen.*

*The Priest adds*
The Lord has put away all your sins.

*Penitent* Thanks be to God.

*The Priest concludes*
Go (*or* abide) in peace, and pray for me, a sinner.

☩

# Preparing for the Rite of Reconciliation

*Set aside a space of time for self-examination. Ask the Holy Spirit to guide you and to give you an awareness not only of the dimensions of your sinfulness, but also an awareness of God's compassion and mercy. Here it is important to make a distinction between self-examination and self-scrutiny. The former is carried out under the guidance of the Holy Spirit and has the compassionate face of Christ as its focus. The latter, which is self-generated, can lead to a preoccupation with our faults and failings that occludes an awareness of God's loving desire to forgive us and to set us free from guilt and shame.*

✠

## A Prayer of Preparation

Spirit of truth and source of love
open my eyes and let me see myself
as God sees and knows me.
Help me to recognize
the disordered affections and desires of my heart;
my whispering sins and my shouting sins,
things done and left undone.

Above all, give me an awareness of God's
boundless compassion and generous mercy
which surpass all I can ask or imagine.
This I pray in the name of the One who came
among us as savior, not as judge.
Amen.

## Aids to Self Examination
*The summary of the law – Mark 12:29-31*

Jesus said, "The first commandment is, 'Hear, O
Israel: the Lord our God, the Lord is one; you shall
love the Lord your God with all your heart, and
with all your soul, and with all your mind, and with
all your strength.' The second is this, 'You shall
love your neighbor as yourself.' There is no other
commandment greater than these."

*The parable of the prodigal son – Luke 15:11-24*

Jesus said, "There was a man who had two sons. The younger of them said to his father, 'Father, give me the share of the property that will belong to me.' So he divided his property between them. A few days later the younger son gathered all he had and traveled to a distant country, and there he squandered his property in dissolute living. When he had spent everything, a severe famine took place throughout that country, and he began to be in need. So he went and hired himself out to one of the citizens of that country, who sent him to his fields to feed the pigs. He would gladly have filled himself with the pods that the pigs were eating; and no one gave him anything. But when he came to himself he said, 'How many of my father's hired hands have bread enough and to spare, but here I am dying of hunger! I will get up and go to my father, and I will say to him, "Father, I have sinned against heaven and before you; I am no longer worthy to be called your son; treat me like one of your hired hands."' So he set off and went to his father. But while he was still far off, his father saw him and was filled with compassion; he ran and put his arms around him and kissed him. Then the son said to him, 'Father, I have sinned against heaven and before you; I am no longer worthy to be called your son.' But the father said to his slaves, 'Quickly, bring out a robe—the best one—and put it on him; put a ring on his finger and sandals on his feet. And get the fatted calf and kill it, and let us eat and celebrate; for this son of mine was dead and is alive again; he was lost and is found!' And they began to celebrate."

## A Prayer of Repentance - Psalm 51:1–18

Have mercy on me, O God, according to your
loving-kindness; *
  in your great compassion blot out my offenses.

Wash me through and through from my wickedness *
  and cleanse me from my sin.

For I know my transgressions, *
  and my sin is ever before me.

Against you only have I sinned *
  and done what is evil in your sight.

And so you are justified when you speak *
	and upright in your judgment.

Indeed, I have been wicked from my birth, *
	a sinner from my mother's womb.

For behold, you look for truth deep within me, *
	and will make me understand wisdom secretly.

Purge me from my sin, and I shall be pure; *
	wash me, and I shall be clean indeed.

Make me hear of joy and gladness, *
	that the body you have broken may rejoice.

Hide your face from my sins *
	and blot out all my iniquities.

Create in me a clean heart, O God, *
	and renew a right spirit within me.

Cast me not away from your presence *
	and take not your holy Spirit from me.

Give me the joy of your saving help again *
	and sustain me with your bountiful Spirit.

I shall teach your ways to the wicked, *
  and sinners shall return to you.

Deliver me from death, O God, *
  and my tongue shall sing of your righteousness,
  O God of my salvation.

Open my lips, O Lord, *
  and my mouth shall proclaim your praise.

Had you desired it, I would have offered sacrifice, *
  but you take no delight in burnt-offerings.

The sacrifice of God is a troubled spirit; *
  a broken and contrite heart, O God, you will
    not despise.


QUESTIONS FOR REFLECTION

How central to my life is my desire to discern and
  fulfill God's loving purpose for me?

Am I open to becoming ever more the person God
  created me to be?

Have I betrayed the dignity I have been given as a
  child of God?

How have I used and misused the gifts and talents
     God has given me?
How have I responded to the opportunities for
     witness and service that have been set before me?
Have I given witness to God's love in my
     relationships?
Am I ready to receive God's mercy and forgiveness?

✠

## A MEDITATION ON GOD'S COMPASSION

*As we examine ourselves we may have to confront our
resistance to God's compassion, and our tendency to cling
instead to the dark comfort of our self-judgment. The interior
struggle between Christ's insistent love and our resistance is
described by George Herbert in his poem entitled "Love."
Love in the poem is the person of the risen Christ. The
"meat" he offers is his reconciling and healing love, which
comes to us in many forms including the Bread and Wine
of the eucharist.*

*Love*

Love bade me welcome: yet my soul drew back,
    Guilty of dust and sin.
But quick-ey'd Love, observing me grow slack
    From my first entrance in,
Drew nearer to me, sweetly questioning,
    If I lack'd any thing.

A guest, I answer'd worthy to be here:
    Love said, you shall be he.
I the unkind, ungrateful? Ah my dear,
    I cannot look on thee.
Love took my hand, and smiling did reply,
    Who made the eyes but I?

Truth Lord, but I have marr'd them: let my shame
    Go where it doth deserve.
And know you not, says Love, who bore the blame?
    My dear, then I will serve.
You must sit down, says Love, and taste my meat:
    So I did sit and eat.

## THANKSGIVING AFTER RECONCILIATION

Give thanks to the LORD, for he is good; *
    his mercy endures for ever.

Let Israel now proclaim, *
    "His mercy endures for ever."

Let the house of Aaron now proclaim, *
    "His mercy endures for ever."

Let those who fear the LORD now proclaim, *
    "His mercy endures for ever."

The LORD is my strength and my song, *
    and he has become my salvation.

"You are my God, and I will thank you; *
    you are my God, and I will exalt you."

Give thanks to the LORD, for he is good; *
    his mercy endures for ever.

*From Psalm 118*

# IV

# I Treasure Your Word in My Heart

*Praying with Scripture*

It is difficult to imagine the depth of the desolation that must have overtaken Jesus' disciples after he was nailed to the cross and put to death. It was three days later that two disciples, in that still grief-stricken state, were encountered by a stranger on the road to Emmaus. As we learn in the twenty-fourth chapter of the Gospel of Luke, the stranger was none other than the risen Christ, though the disciples were unable to recognize him. He then proceeded, beginning with Moses and the prophets, to interpret "the things about himself in all the scriptures." Only later, in the breaking of the bread, did they recognize him as the One they thought they had lost, and exclaim: "Were not our hearts burning *within us. . .while he was opening the scriptures to us?"*

*Later the risen Christ appears to the disciples gathered in Jerusalem, and again we are told that he "opened their minds to understand the scriptures."*

*These resurrection encounters teach us that the risen Christ is the Lord of scripture and reveals himself to us through its words. Put another way, Christ the Word (with a capital W) stands at the heart of the scriptural word. Scripture, therefore, has a sacramental character in that it mediates and reveals the presence of the risen Christ.*

*The Letter to the Hebrews tells us that the word of God is "living and active, sharper than any two-edged sword, piercing until it divides soul from spirit, joints from marrow. It is able to judge the thoughts and intentions of the heart." Divine address takes many forms, as scripture itself reveals. History and myth, prose and poetry can all be the medium of God's self-revelation. "I treasure your word in my heart," the psalmist cries, aware that scripture is a form of God's intimate address.*

*Have you ever had the experience of reading or hearing a passage of scripture that you have read or heard many* times before but now it comes to life in a new way? At such moments Christ may be addressing us in a specific verse or passage, thereby illumining our minds, encouraging our hearts and drawing us more deeply into companionship. The passage becomes God's word to us right then and there. Indeed, when this happens our hearts do burn within us.

As we approach a particular passage of scripture we sometimes find ourselves asking if it is literally true. We wonder: did this really happen the way it is described? Would a loving God have actually commanded or done this? Here it is helpful to keep in mind that the answers to these questions are not simply Yes or No, True or False. Rather, we must look at what early commentators called different levels of meaning and different ways of approaching scripture. A distinction was often made between a "literal" reading and a "spiritual" reading.

An example is to be found in the Song of Mary in the Gospel of Luke.

✠

Mary said,

"My soul magnifies the Lord,

and my spirit rejoices in God my Savior,

for he has looked with favor on the lowliness of his
servant.

Surely, from now on all generations will call me
blessed;

for the Mighty One has done great things for me,
and holy is his name.

His mercy is for those who fear him from generation
to generation.

He has shown strength with his arm;

he has scattered the proud in the thoughts of their
hearts.

He has brought down the powerful from their
thrones,

and lifted up the lowly;

he has filled the hungry with good things,

and sent the rich away empty. He has helped his
servant Israel,

in remembrance of his mercy,

according to the promise he made to our ancestors,

to Abraham and to his descendants forever."

✠

We might ask if this was actually what Mary said. We might wonder who was present to record her song. We might further note that her song bears a remarkable likeness to the Song of Hannah in the First Book of Samuel. At the same time, we can give Mary's words the freedom to address us on their own terms, in which case Mary's humble rejoicing can become our own. The spiritual power of Mary's words takes us well beyond questions of historical accuracy.

To allow scripture to speak to us on its own terms is to allow Christ to address us in his own way. Just as he used such an unlikely medium as mud to heal a man born blind, so too, Christ, through the agency of the Holy Spirit, can use an unlikely passage of scripture to overcome the blindness of our hearts.

One of the gifts of the Book of Common Prayer is the Daily Office Lectionary, which provides us with an ordered way of allowing Christ to encounter us through the scriptural word. Rather than returning again and again to favorite passages, we make room for the full sweep of scripture to break upon us and have its way with us.

There have been countless moments in my own life when what had been a remote passage of scripture leapt to life and became a living word because of what was going on at the time. For example, many years ago while I was a parish priest I was giving a clergy conference before the beginning of Lent. My topic was the need for balanced lives of prayer, work, and recreation. I said to the priests that one of the temptations for the ordained was the tendency to overwork. Ironically, I was giving this lecture on my day off. Worse yet, when the meeting ended I rushed off because I had to catch a train in order to keep an appointment to discuss the baptism of a parishioner's son.

As I arrived at the railway station, the train was just pulling away from the platform. I ran to catch it and as I did so I felt a sharp pain in my heel. Within an hour I was in a hospital bed awaiting surgery. In addition to being upset and frustrated about the accident I was angry and I blamed myself for my stupidity.

As evening came, I read Evening Prayer and the psalm appointed was Psalm 94, which had never particularly spoken to me. As I read verse 18 the psalm came to life: As often as I said, "My foot has slipped" your love, O Lord, upheld me.

Suddenly, my frustration and anger at myself dissolved and I began to laugh. I no longer was alone but felt embraced by Christ who, through the words of the psalm, was saying to me: I am with you in this. Stop judging yourself. In the future don't try to do more than I am asking you to do! What had begun as a trial and a burden became a season of unexpected grace and blessing.

In this event several dimensions of the word came together. The circumstances of my life brought about a fresh reading of a familiar psalm. This in turn brought forth a dimension of Christ's presence implanted deep within me which became Christ's living word to me right then and there.

✣

As you pray with scripture, whether the passage is as appointed in the lectionary or something you have chosen, let the text speak directly to you. Even parts of scripture that may be myth or fable can be used by the Holy Spirit to address us and draw us into union with God in Christ. The gospels, especially the Gospel of John, invite us into companionship with Jesus as disciples, a word which means a learner: that is, one who is ready to hear and receive the word.

## A Prayer as You Begin

Lord Jesus Christ, you are the Word incarnate
and my true teacher.
Let your Spirit be present as I read and reflect upon
your word.
Open my heart and mind to understand your
revelation,
that I may be rooted and grounded in your love,
and grow into your likeness.  Amen.

*Choose a passage of scripture and read it aloud, slowly. Invite Christ to meet you with his Spirit in the passage you have read. It is helpful to have a study Bible at hand as its explanatory notes and commentary can help situate you in relation to the passage. Do not, however, strain to find meaning. Let the Spirit impart what the Spirit wishes to impart.*

## An Example

*The following passage from the Book of Isaiah, in its historical context, is a prophecy about the redemption and restoration of Israel after a time of exile. It can, however, be read in immediate and personal terms. In this passage you are Jacob. You are Israel. You might read the passage aloud twice, the second time inserting your own name.*

☩

But now thus says the Lord, he who created you, O Jacob, he who formed you, O Israel: Do not fear, for I have redeemed you; I have called you by name, you are mine. When you pass through the waters, I will be with you; and through the rivers, they shall not overwhelm you; when you walk through fire you shall not be burned, and the flame shall not consume you. For I am the Lord your God, the Holy One of Israel, your Savior.

*Isaiah 43:1-3*

☩

Reflect upon the fact that God has formed you and called you by name as an act of God's creative love.

Ask the Holy Spirit to bring to you awareness of how being called and named – being shaped and fashioned – has taken place in the seasons and events of your life.

What events, challenges, joys, and particular persons have played a role making me who I am today?

What times of struggle and testing, loss and suffering, what "rivers and flames" have I had to pass through?

In what ways has God been present, giving me courage, endurance, or hope?

How has the Christ companioned me over the years?

How is Christ companioning me in this present moment?

The fruit of your encounter with scripture may appear then as you pray with the text or it may appear only later, often when you least expect it and most need it. If you find yourself straining for results as you ponder these questions, you might make use of the following psalm verse to maintain your ability to wait upon the leading of the Spirit with patience. After all, the Spirit is free to blow where the Spirit wills and not according to our sense of urgency.

✠

For God **alone** my soul in silence waits; from him comes my salvation.

*Psalm 62:1*

✠

*When you conclude your encounter with the text, give thanks to God for the time spent in the company of the word.*

✠

*The psalms are a rich resource from which to draw, as they contain the full range of human emotions: from joy and confidence to anger and despair, sometimes within the same psalm. Taken as a whole, the psalms represent the interplay of the Holy Spirit and our human spirit. Here are several psalms with which you may choose to pray.*

✠

*Psalm 31 – A song in time of affliction*

In you, O Lord, have I taken refuge;
let me never be put to shame; *
     deliver me in your righteousness.

Incline your ear to me; *
     make haste to deliver me.

Be my strong rock, a castle to keep me safe,
for you are my crag and my stronghold; *
     for the sake of your Name, lead me and guide me.

Take me out of the net that they have secretly set for me, *
     for you are my tower of strength.

Into your hands I commend my spirit, *
     for you have redeemed me,
          O Lord, O God of truth.

I hate those who cling to worthless idols, *
     and I put my trust in the Lord.

I will rejoice and be glad because of your mercy; *
     for you have seen my affliction;
          you know my distress.

You have not shut me up in the power of the enemy; *
    you have set my feet in an open place.

Have mercy on me, O Lord, for I am in trouble; *
    my eye is consumed with sorrow,
    and also my throat and my belly.

For my life is wasted with grief,
and my years with sighing; *
    my strength fails me because of affliction,
    and my bones are consumed.

I have become a reproach to all my enemies and
            even to my neighbors,
    a dismay to those of my acquaintance; *
    when they see me in the street they avoid me.

I am forgotten like a dead man, out of mind; *
    I am as useless as a broken pot.

For I have heard the whispering of the crowd;
fear is all around; *
    they put their heads together against me;
    they plot to take my life.

But as for me, I have trusted in you, O LORD. *
I have said, "You are my God.

My times are in your hand; *
rescue me from the hand of my enemies,
and from those who persecute me.

Make your face to shine upon your servant, *
and in your loving-kindness save me."

LORD, let me not be ashamed for having called
upon you; *
rather, let the wicked be put to shame;
let them be silent in the grave.

Let the lying lips be silenced which speak against
the righteous, *
haughtily, disdainfully, and with contempt.

How great is your goodness, O LORD!
which you have laid up for those who fear you; *
which you have done in the sight of all
for those who put their trust in you.

You hide them in the covert of your presence from
those who slander them; *
you keep them in your shelter from the strife
of tongues.

Blessed be the LORD! *
for he has shown me the wonders of his love in a
besieged city.

Yet I said in my alarm,
"I have been cut off from the sight of your eyes." *
Nevertheless, you heard the sound of my entreaty
when I cried out to you.

Love the LORD, all you who worship him; *
the LORD protects the faithful,
but repays to the full those who act haughtily.

Be strong and let your heart take courage, *
all you who wait for the LORD.

✠

*Psalm 40 – A song of thanksgiving*

I waited patiently upon the LORD; *
>    he stooped to me and heard my cry.

He lifted me out of the desolate pit, out of the mire
>        and clay; *
>    he set my feet upon a high cliff and made my
>        footing sure.

He put a new song in my mouth,
a song of praise to our God; *
>    many shall see, and stand in awe,
>        and put their trust in the LORD.

Happy are they who trust in the LORD! *
>    they do not resort to evil spirits or turn to false gods.

Great things are they that you have done, O LORD
>        my God!
how great your wonders and your plans for us! *
>    there is none who can be compared with you.

Oh, that I could make them known and tell them! *
>    but they are more than I can count.

In sacrifice and offering you take no pleasure *
    (you have given me ears to hear you);

Burnt-offering and sin-offering you have not required, *
    and so I said, "Behold, I come.

In the roll of the book it is written concerning me: *
    'I love to do your will, O my God;
your law is deep in my heart.'"

I proclaimed righteousness in the great congregation; *
    behold, I did not restrain my lips;
    and that, O LORD, you know.

Your righteousness have I not hidden in my heart;
I have spoken of your faithfulness and your
        deliverance; *
    I have not concealed your love and faithfulness
        from the great congregation.

You are the LORD;
do not withhold your compassion from me; *
    let your love and your faithfulness keep me safe
        for ever,

For innumerable troubles have crowded upon me;
my sins have overtaken me, and I cannot see; *
    they are more in number than the hairs of my head,
    and my heart fails me.

Be pleased, O Lord, to deliver me; *
    O Lord, make haste to help me.

Let them be ashamed and altogether dismayed
who seek after my life to destroy it; *
    let them draw back and be disgraced
    who take pleasure in my misfortune.

Let those who say "Aha!" and gloat over me be
            confounded, *
    because they are ashamed.

Let all who seek you rejoice in you and be glad; *
    let those who love your salvation continually say,
    "Great is the Lord!"

Though I am poor and afflicted, *
    the Lord will have regard for me.

You are my helper and my deliverer; *
    do not tarry, O my God.

Psalm 51:1-18 – *A song of penitence* (See page 82.)

Psalm 104 – *A song of creation*

Bless the LORD, O my soul; *
    O LORD my God, how excellent is your greatness!
    you are clothed with majesty and splendor.

You wrap yourself with light as with a cloak *
    and spread out the heavens like a curtain.

You lay the beams of your chambers in the waters
        above; *
    you make the clouds your chariot;
    you ride on the wings of the wind.

You make the winds your messengers *
    and flames of fire your servants.

You have set the earth upon its foundations, *
    so that it never shall move at any time.

You covered it with the Deep as with a mantle; *

    the waters stood higher than the mountains.

At your rebuke they fled; *

    at the voice of your thunder they hastened away.

They went up into the hills and down to the valleys
        beneath, *

    to the places you had appointed for them.

You set the limits that they should not pass; *

    they shall not again cover the earth.

You send the springs into the valleys; *

    they flow between the mountains.

All the beasts of the field drink their fill from them, *

    and the wild asses quench their thirst.

Beside them the birds of the air make their nests *

    and sing among the branches.

You water the mountains from your dwelling on high; *

    the earth is fully satisfied by the fruit of your works.

You make grass grow for flocks and herds *

    and plants to serve mankind;

That they may bring forth food from the earth, *
　　and wine to gladden our hearts,

Oil to make a cheerful countenance, *
　　and bread to strengthen the heart.

The trees of the LORD are full of sap, *
　　the cedars of Lebanon which he planted,

In which the birds build their nests, *
　　and in whose tops the stork makes his dwelling.

The high hills are a refuge for the mountain goats, *
　　and the stony cliffs for the rock badgers.

You appointed the moon to mark the seasons, *
　　and the sun knows the time of its setting.

You make darkness that it may be night, *
　　in which all the beasts of the forest prowl.

The lions roar after their prey *
　　and seek their food from God.

The sun rises, and they slip away *
　　and lay themselves down in their dens.

Man goes forth to his work *
    and to his labor until the evening.

O LORD, how manifold are your works! *
    in wisdom you have made them all;
    the earth is full of your creatures.

Yonder is the great and wide sea
with its living things too many to number, *
    creatures both small and great.

There move the ships,
and there is that Leviathan, *
    which you have made for the sport of it.

All of them look to you *
    to give them their food in due season.

You give it to them; they gather it; *
    you open your hand, and they are filled with
        good things.

You hide your face, and they are terrified; *
    you take away their breath,
    and they die and return to their dust.

You send forth your Spirit, and they are created; *
    and so you renew the face of the earth.

May the glory of the LORD endure for ever; *
    may the LORD rejoice in all his works.

He looks at the earth and it trembles; *
    he touches the mountains and they smoke.

I will sing to the LORD as long as I live; *
    I will praise my God while I have my being.

May these words of mine please him; *
    I will rejoice in the LORD.

Let sinners be consumed out of the earth, *
    and the wicked be no more.

Bless the LORD, O my soul. *
    Hallelujah!

☩

*Psalm 139 – A song of God's presence*

LORD, you have searched me out and known me; *
    you know my sitting down and my rising up;
    you discern my thoughts from afar.

You trace my journeys and my resting-places *
    and are acquainted with all my ways.

Indeed, there is not a word on my lips, *
    but you, O LORD, know it altogether.

You press upon me behind and before *
    and lay your hand upon me.

Such knowledge is too wonderful for me; *
    it is so high that I cannot attain to it.

Where can I go then from your Spirit? *
    where can I flee from your presence?

If I climb up to heaven, you are there; *
    if I make the grave my bed, you are there also.

If I take the wings of the morning *
    and dwell in the uttermost parts of the sea,

Even there your hand will lead me *
    and your right hand hold me fast.

If I say, "Surely the darkness will cover me, *
    and the light around me turn to night,"

Darkness is not dark to you;
the night is as bright as the day; *
    darkness and light to you are both alike.

For you yourself created my inmost parts; *
    you knit me together in my mother's womb.

I will thank you because I am marvelously made; *
    your works are wonderful, and I know it well.

My body was not hidden from you, *
    while I was being made in secret
    and woven in the depths of the earth.

Your eyes beheld my limbs, yet unfinished in the womb;
all of them were written in your book; *
    they were fashioned day by day,
    when as yet there was none of them.

How deep I find your thoughts, O God! *
    how great is the sum of them!

If I were to count them, they would be more in
number than the sand; *
to count them all, my life span would need to
be like yours.

Oh, that you would slay the wicked, O God! *
You that thirst for blood, depart from me.

They speak despitefully against you; *
your enemies take your Name in vain.

Do I not hate those, O LORD, who hate you? *
and do I not loathe those who rise up against you?

I hate them with a perfect hatred; *
they have become my own enemies.

Search me out, O God, and know my heart; *
try me and know my restless thoughts.

Look well whether there be any wickedness in me *
and lead me in the way that is everlasting.

⊹

*Psalm 150 – A song of praise* (See page 70.)

# Seasons of the Year

*The Church Year presents us with the opportunity to grow in companionship with Christ as we accompany him through the gospel and the outpouring of the Holy Spirit at Pentecost into the life and struggles of the community that formed in Christ's name. The following brief passages are provided to help you enter into the spirit of each season. In addition, you might want to meditate upon the readings appointed for Sundays and weekdays in the Lectionary.*

## Advent

Jesus said, "Keep awake — for you do not know when the master of the house will come, in the evening, or at midnight, or at cockcrow, or at dawn, or else he may find you asleep when he comes suddenly. And what I say to you I say to all: Keep awake." *Mark 13:35-37*

## Christmas

The Word became flesh and lived among us, and we have seen his glory, the glory as of a father's only son, full of grace and truth. . . . From his fullness we have all received, grace upon grace. *John 1:14,16*

## Epiphany

Jesus said, "I am the light of the world. Whoever follows me will never walk in darkness but will have the light of life." *John 8:12*

## Lent

Return to the Lord your God, for he is gracious and merciful, slow to anger, and abounding in steadfast love, and relents from punishing. *Joel 2:13*

## Holy Week

Christ himself bore our sins in his body on the cross, so that, free from sins, we might live for righteousness; by his wounds you have been healed. *1 Peter 2:24*

## Easter

If you have been raised with Christ, seek the things that are above where Christ is, seated at the right hand of God. Set your mind on things that are above, not on things that are on earth, for you have died, and your life is hidden with Christ in God. *Colossians 3:1-3*


## Pentecost

The fruit of the Spirit is love, joy, peace, patience, kindness, generosity, gentleness, faithfulness, and self-control. . . . If we live by the Spirit, let us also be guided by the Spirit. *Galatians 5:22,25*

✝

# Scripture and Common Prayer

*The reading of scripture is an integral part of the various liturgies of the church and is another way in which the Spirit can cause our hearts to burn within us. Jesus says in the gospel that when two or three are gathered together in his name, "I am there among them." One of the ways Jesus is present is in the proclamation of the word in the course of the liturgical assembly. When we hear the word read aloud in the company of others, we are being addressed both personally and as limbs and members of Christ's risen body bound together through baptism. At such times new dimensions of the word can reveal themselves and speak directly to our hearts.*

*The function of the sermon or homily in the course of public worship is to break the bread of the word so that it can nourish and strengthen the community in its life of witness and service. In the course of our worship the care with which the words of scripture are proclaimed, and our own readiness to hear and receive them, can make the difference between the word falling on barren soil or finding root and bearing fruit.*

## Reading the Bible with Others

*Here again, when two or three are gathered together around the word Christ is present among them. Pondering the scripture with others makes it possible for us to encounter different dimensions of the word as they are drawn forth from those engaged in searching the scriptures together.*

*In the Gospel of John, Jesus says to his disciples, "I still have many things to say to you, but you cannot bear them now. When the Spirit of truth comes, he will guide you into all the truth. . . . He will take what is mine and declare it to you." The truth Christ seeks to convey to us is larger than any one person's perspective. In order to know the truth as revealed in Christ, we must seek it together. Each of us who has been baptized into Christ bears some dimension of that larger truth which is found in Christ himself. Thus, we discover truth in communion with others. The insights offered by others as we search the scriptures can expand and enrich our capacity to discern the truth. As Jesus tells us: "I am the way, the truth and the life." The truth in its fullness, therefore, is not simply a body of information but the person of Jesus himself.*

†

**A Prayer before Bible Study with Others**
Lord Jesus Christ,
    you are the way, the truth, and the life.
You are the Word at the heart of the word.
Send your Spirit of truth among us
    as we gather together to search the scriptures.
Help me to listen to the opinions and insights
        of others
    with an open heart and mind.
Help me to perceive dimensions of your truth
        present in each of us
    who have been baptized into your risen body.
Speak, Lord, for your servant is listening.
Amen.

✠ ✠ ✠ ✠ ✠

# V

# The Communion of Saints

*A Fellowship of Love and Prayer*

*In the Apostles' Creed we proclaim, "I believe in the Communion of Saints." In so doing we acknowledge that we are supported and sustained by a vast fellowship of love and prayer. The men and women who have gone before us and passed through the door of death continue to be present with us.*

*We often think of saints as those who have been officially acknowledged by the church for their exemplary lives. However, participation in the Communion of Saints is not reserved for those who have been formally declared saints by the church or commemorated in the church's calendar. In the New Testament the term "saint" is broadly applied to all who belong to the community of faith. A family member,*

*a teacher, a friend, the companion of one's heart may have
touched our lives in such a way that they continue beyond
death to be an inspiration, a guide, and a source of blessing.
The Holy Spirit, who is the minister of communion, binds us
together in a relationship that remains unbroken by death.*

*A prayer from those appointed for the Burial of the Dead
in the Book of Common Prayer underscores the fact that
God's "righteous servants" are more than examples. They
are friends and companions in Christ who can be called
upon to pray for us, just as we can ask others in this life to
remember us in their prayers.*

☩

O God, the King of saints, we praise and glorify your
holy Name for all your servants who have finished their
course in your faith and fear: for the blessed Virgin Mary;
for the holy patriarchs, prophets, apostles, and martyrs;
and for all your other righteous servants, known to us
and unknown; and we pray that, encouraged by their
examples, aided by their prayers, and strengthened
by their fellowship, we also may be partakers of the
inheritance of the saints in light; through the merits of
your Son Jesus Christ our Lord.  Amen.

☩

Just as we may ask those who have gone before us in the Communion of Saints to pray for us, so too we pray for the departed, asking God that "increasing in knowledge and love of thee they may go from strength to strength in the life of perfect service in thy heavenly kingdom."

These words from the Prayer Book help us to think of life beyond the grave as a new mode of being. It can be understood as a new season of continuing growth and discovery, and of moving from "strength to strength." The eternal rest we ask God to grant to the departed, therefore, is not some sort of static slumber, but an ongoing journey into the unfathomable depths of God's eternal love. In the light of God's love they enter into the deep truth of who they are called to be, which is how they are known by God. St. Augustine tells us that we are a mystery to ourselves, and that God alone knows who we are.

And, as St. Paul tells us, we "now see in a mirror dimly" and "now know only in part." It is only on the other side of death that, freed from this partial vision, we will know ourselves even as we have been fully known by God. It is with confidence in this larger vision that we remember the departed.

# Prayers for the Departed

O God, whose mercies cannot be numbered: Accept our prayers on behalf of your servant _____ and grant *him* an entrance into the land of light and joy, in the fellowship of your saints; through Jesus Christ our Lord, who lives and reigns with you and the Holy Spirit, one God, now and for ever. Amen.

☩

Give rest, O Christ, to your servant _____ with your saints, where sorrow and pain are no more, neither sighing, but life everlasting. Amen.

☩

Rest eternal grant to _____, O Lord;
And let light perpetual shine upon *her*.
And may *her* soul, and the souls of all the departed, through the mercy of God, rest in peace. Amen.

☩

✠

Lord God,

we can hope for others nothing better

than the happiness we desire for ourselves.

Therefore, I pray you, do not separate me after death

from those I have loved on earth.

Grant that where I am they may be with me,

and that I may enjoy their presence in heaven

after being deprived of it on earth.

Receive your beloved children ( _____ and _____ )

into your life-giving heart.

And after this brief life on earth, give them eternal

happiness.  Amen.

*After St. Ambrose, 397*

✠

✠

Eternal and ever-living God,

let your deathless love embrace and heal

those who have gone before us, especially _____.

May *she* go from strength to strength in your service

and grow in knowledge and love of you.

And, in the days to come, may the bonds of love and companionship

we knew in this life

continue in ways that accord with your will;

through our Savior, Jesus Christ, who is the

resurrection and the life

now and for ever.

Amen.

✠

✠

God of mercy and source of all goodness,
Grant to those who have departed this life
    a place with your saints in your eternal dwelling.
Remember *my parents*, _____ *and* _____ , *and the*
    *other members of my family I now call to mind . . .*
Forgive their sins and shortcomings,
    and draw them
    with the bands of your deathless love
    into life in all its fullness.
Make their joy complete,
    and in your light may they see light;
through Jesus Christ,
    who dispels all darkness
    and overcomes the shadow of death.
Amen.

✠

*In times of grief and loss we can gain strength and find consolation by drawing upon words of scripture. A sentence or a phrase repeated and held in our consciousness can become the door through which the risen Christ can enter and companion us, just as he companioned his grief-stricken disciples on the road to Emmaus. Here are some passages you may choose to use:*

Jesus said. . . "I am the resurrection and the life. Those who believe in me, even though they die, will live, and everyone who lives and believes in me will never die." *John 11:25*

Jesus said. . . "Do not let your hearts be troubled. Believe in God, believe also in me. In my Father's house there are many dwelling places. If it were not so, would I have told you that I go to prepare a place for you? I will come again and will take you to myself, so that where I am, there you may be also." *John 14:1-3*

✠

*St. Paul said.* . . "For I am convinced that neither death, nor life, nor angels, nor rulers, nor things present, nor things to come, nor powers, nor height, nor depth, nor anything else in all creation, will be able to separate us from the love of God in Jesus Christ our Lord. *Romans 8:38-39*

✠

They will hunger no more, and thirst no more;
the sun will not strike them, nor any scorching heat;
for the Lamb at the center of the throne will be their
   shepherd,
and he will guide them to springs of the water of life,
and God will wipe away every tear from their eyes.
*Revelation 7:16-18*

✠

The LORD is my shepherd;

> I shall not be in want.

Though I walk through the valley of the shadow
> of death,

I shall fear no evil;

> For you are with me;

> Your rod and your staff, they comfort me.

*From Psalm 23*

# The Mother of Jesus

*Since the early centuries of the Common Era, the Blessed Virgin Mary has occupied a special place in the liturgical and devotional life of the church by virtue of her unique role in the Incarnation. She has been regarded as the image of faithful availability to God's word, as demanding and inscrutable as that word at times might be. In faith, Mary followed her son to the foot of the cross where, in accordance with Simeon's prophecy recorded in the Gospel of Luke, her* soul was pierced by the sword of suffering. She has become, therefore, a model of costly discipleship for Christians personally and for the church as a whole.

By the time of the Reformation, in many quarters in the West, devotion to Mary had displaced devotion to her son. The corrective on the part of the Reformers was drastic: an almost total suppression of the one who had said, "Surely, from now on all generations will call me blessed."

✠

The Anglican tradition has always held Mary in high regard, but has been restrained with respect to devotion to her or asking for her prayers. We sing in praise of Mary's faithfulness in a familiar hymn: O higher than the cherubim, more glorious than the seraphim. . . Thou bearer of the eternal Word, most gracious, magnify the Lord. At the same time, the following from a poem by George Herbert captures something of the tension felt by many between high regard and restraint in seeking Mary's aid.

*To All Angels and Saints*

Not out of envy or maliciousness
Do I forbear to crave your special aid:
    I would you address
My vows to thee most gladly, blessed Maid,
And Mother of my God, in my distress.


Thou art the holy mine, whence came the gold,
The great restorative for all decay
    In young and old;
Thou art the cabinet where the jewel lay:
Chiefly to thee would I my soul unfold:


But now (alas!) I dare not; for our King,
Whom we do all jointly adore and praise,
    Bids no such thing:
And where his pleasure no injunction lays,
('Tis your own case) ye never move a wing.


⳨

With reform in Marian devotion in the Roman Catholic Church and a renewed appreciation of the Communion of Saints, Anglicanism and churches of the Reformation have begun to recover a devotion to Mary in which she is seen not only as God's humble servant and a loving mother, but as sister and companion and woman of courage. Her song, recorded in the Gospel of Luke, is an outburst of both humility and prophetic judgment. (See the Song of Mary, page 92.)

✠

In addition to the Hail Mary and Regina Coeli (pages 21-24) here are several other prayers addressed to the Mother of Jesus in which we seek the support of her companionship and prayer.

✠

Rejoice, O Mother of God and Maiden, Mary full of grace, the Lord is with you.

✠

You are blessed among women, and blessed is the fruit of your womb, for you have given birth to the Savior of our souls.

✛

Pray for me that by sharing in the suffering of your son I may know the power of his resurrection. Amen.

*Adapted from an Eastern Orthodox prayer*

✛

Hail to you, Mary, Mother!
You are full of loving grace,
The Lord God is always with you,
Blessed are you, Mary, among women,
Blessed is the fruit of your womb, Jesus,
Blessed are you, Queen of Grace;
Holy Mary, Mother of Jesus,
Pray for me a sinner,
Now and at the hour of death.

*A Celtic prayer*

✠

Mary, our sister,
Mother of the Word Incarnate:
    your faithfulness led you to the foot of the cross
    where your soul was pierced by the sword
        of suffering.
Pray for us that your courage and endurance
        may find a home in our hearts,
    and let your loving intercession embrace all
       those who grieve
    and bear the wound of loss.
Amen.

✠

# Supported by Their Prayer

*At various points in my life, particular men and women within this fellowship of love and prayer, through the example of their lives, have imparted wisdom and shed light upon the way. I had the sense that they were sent by the Holy Spirit to be companions of my soul. In such moments I have expressed gratitude for their companionship and asked them for their prayers.*

## Prayer in Companionship
## with One's Patron Saint

Lord Jesus Christ, Son of the living God, for the sake of the prayers of your blessed Mother, of ( _____ , *the name of one's patron saint*), of ( _____ , *the saint commemorated on this day*), and of all the saints, have mercy on me, and strengthen me with your grace, for you are ever compassionate and your love embraces the whole of creation.  Amen.

## A Litany of the Saints

*This beginning of a litany of the saints is included as an
example of how you might compose a litany of your own.
The composition of a litany is a way of remembering those
who have gone before, including particularly those in the
communion of saints whose life and witness have inspired
and encouraged you. Leave your litany open to continual ad-
aptation as the Spirit may introduce you to new companions
along the way. The first three invocations are adapted from
the English Litany of 1544.*

Saint Mary, Mother of God
our Savior, Jesus Christ: *Pray for us*

All holy Angels and Archangels,
and all orders of blessed spirits: *Pray for us*

All holy Patriarchs and Matriarchs,
Prophets, Apostles, Martyrs,
and all the blessed company of heaven: *Pray for us*

Peter and Paul: *Pray for us*
Hildegard of Bingen: *Pray for us*

Francis and Clare: *Pray for us*

George Herbert: *Pray for us*

Absalom Jones: *Pray for us*

William Wilberforce: *Pray for us*

Evelyn Underhill: *Pray for us*

Jonathan Daniels: *Pray for us*

Constance and your companions: *Pray for us*

[ _____ ]: *Pray for us. . .*

*You might conclude your litany with the following prayer:*

Almighty God, by your Holy Spirit you have made us one with your saints in heaven and on earth: Grant that in our earthly pilgrimage we may always be supported by this fellowship of love and prayer, and know ourselves to be surrounded by their witness to your power and mercy. We ask this for the sake of Jesus Christ, in whom all our intercessions are acceptable through the Spirit, and who lives and reigns for ever and ever. Amen.

✠

# Praying with the Saints

*Many in this fellowship of love and prayer have composed prayers of their own. Over the years their words and aspirations have nourished and enriched the prayer of countless others. Here are some that may nourish your prayer as well.*

## Prayer of Self-Offering

Take, Lord,
and receive all my liberty,
my memory, my understanding
and my entire will,
all that I have and possess.
You have given all to me,
to you, Lord, I return it.
All is yours;
do with it what you will.
Give me only your love
and your grace,
that is enough for me.

*St. Ignatius of Loyola, 1556*

## In God's Service

Teach us, good Lord, to serve you as you deserve, to give and not to count the cost, to fight and not to heed the wounds, to toil and not to seek for rest, to labor and not to ask for any reward, save that of knowing that we do your will; through Jesus Christ our Lord. Amen.

*St. Ignatius of Loyola*

☩

Almighty God, give us wisdom to perceive you,
intellect to understand you,
diligence to seek you,
patience to wait for you,
vision to uphold you,
a heart to meditate upon you,
and life to proclaim you.

*St. Benedict, circa 540*

☩

## Prayer of Abandonment

My Father
I abandon myself to you.
Do with me as you will.
Whatever you may do with me
I thank you.
I am ready for all,
I accept all
provided your will is fulfilled in me
and in all your creatures.
I ask for nothing more
my God.
I place my soul in your hands.
I give it to you, my God,
with all the love of my heart
because I love you.
And for me it is a necessity of love,
this gift of myself,
this placing of myself in your hands
without reserve
in boundless confidence,
because you are
my Father.

*Charles de Foucauld, 1916*

†

## A Song of Adoration

God chose to be our mother in all things
    and so made the foundation of his work,
        most humbly and most pure, in the Virgin's womb.
God, the perfect wisdom of all,
    arrayed himself in this humble place.
Christ came in our poor flesh
    to share a mother's care.
Our mothers bear us for pain and for death;
    our true mother, Jesus, bears us for joy and
        endless life.
Christ carried us within him in love and travail,
    until the full time of his passion.
And when all was completed and he had carried us
        so for joy,
    still all this could not satisfy the power of
        his wonderful love.
All that we owe is redeemed in truly loving God,
    for the love of Christ works in us;
    Christ is the one whom we love.

*Julian of Norwich, circa 1417*

✠

## Prayer for Christ's Presence

Christ with me, Christ before me, Christ behind me,

Christ in me, Christ beneath me, Christ above me,

Christ on my right, Christ on my left,

Christ when I lie down, Christ when I sit down,

Christ when I arise,

Christ in the heart of everyone who thinks of me,

Christ in the mouth of everyone who speaks of me,

Christ in the eye of everyone who sees me,

Christ in every ear that hears me.


## Invocation at the Beginning of the Day

✠ I arise today

Through a mighty strength, the invocation of the

Trinity,

Through belief in the threeness,

Through confession of the oneness

of the Creator of Creation.

*Attributed to St. Patrick, 461*

✠

**Prayer for Grace**

O Lord, I do not pray for tasks equal to my strength:
I ask for strength equal to my tasks.

*Phillips Brooks, 1893*

**A Prayer of Thanksgiving**

Thanks be to you, Lord Jesus Christ, for all the
benefits and blessings which you have given me, for
all the pains and insults which you have borne for me.
O most merciful Redeemer, Friend, and Brother, may
I know you more clearly, love you more dearly, and
follow you more nearly, day by day. Amen.

*St. Richard of Chichester, 1253*

## Seeking God

Lord, you speak in my heart and say, "Seek my face." Your face, Lord, will I seek; hide not your face from me. Raise me up from myself and draw me to you. Cleanse, heal, quicken, enlighten the eye of my mind that it may look to you. Strengthen my soul that with all the power of my understanding it may strive to know you: for you are life and wisdom, truth and beauty, and everything that is good. Amen.

*After St. Anselm, 1109*

☩

## A Prayer Attributed to St. Francis

Lord, make me an instrument of your peace. Where there is hatred, let me sow love; where there is injury, pardon; where there is discord, union; where there is doubt, faith; where there is despair, hope; where there is darkness, light; where there is sadness, joy. Grant that I may not so much seek to be consoled as to console; to be understood as to understand; to be loved as to love. For it is in giving that we receive; it is pardoning that we are pardoned; and it is in dying that we are born to eternal life. Amen.

## Canticle of the Creatures

Most High, all powerful, good Lord,
to you be praise, glory, honor and all blessing.

Only to you, Most High, do they belong
and no one is worthy to call upon your name.

May you be praised, my Lord, with all your creatures,
    especially brother sun,
through whom you lighten the day for us.

He is beautiful and radiant with great splendor;
he signifies you, O Most High.

Be praised, my Lord, for sister moon and the stars;
clear and precious and lovely, they are formed in heaven.

Be praised, my Lord, for sister water,
who is very useful and humble and precious and pure.

Be praised, my Lord, for brother fire,
    by whom the night is illumined for us;
he is beautiful and cheerful, full of power and strength.

Be praised, my Lord, for our sister, mother earth,
    who sustains and governs us
and produces diverse fruits
    and colored flowers and grass.

Be praised, my Lord, by all those who forgive for
        love of you
and who bear weakness and tribulation.

Blessed are those who bear them in peace:
for you, Most High, they will be crowned.

Be praised, my Lord, for our sister, the death of the body,
from which no one living is able to flee;
    woe to those who are dying in mortal sin.

Blessed are those who are found doing your
        most holy will,
for the second death will do them no harm.

Praise and bless my Lord and give him thanks
and serve him with great humility.

*St. Francis of Assisi*

## Personal witness

Lord Jesus Christ, make those who love you, and who love you in return, mirrors of you to those who are unloving; that being drawn to your image they may reproduce it in themselves, light reflecting light, love kindling love, until God is all in all. Amen.

*After Christina Rossetti, 1894*

## The Road Ahead of Me

My Lord God,

I have no idea where I am going.

I do not see the road ahead of me.

I cannot know for certain where it will end.

Nor do I really know myself,

and the fact that I think that I am following

    your will does not mean that I am actually doing so.

But I believe that the desire to please you

    does in fact please you.

And I hope that I have that desire in all that

        I am doing.

I hope that I will never do anything apart from

        that desire.

And I know that if I do this,

You will lead me by the right road

    though I may know nothing about it.

Therefore will I trust you always

    though I may seem to be lost in the shadow of death.

I will not fear, for you are ever with me,

And you will never leave me to face my perils alone.

*Thomas Merton, 1968*

✠

## A Prayer for Availability to God's Will

O God, I do not know what to ask of you.

You alone know my true needs

and love me more than I know how to love.

I ask neither for cross nor consolation,

but only that I may discern and do your will.

Teach me to wait in patience with an open heart,

knowing that your ways are not our ways,

and your thoughts are not our thoughts.

Help me to see where I have erected idols of certitude

to defend myself from the demands of your ever

unfolding truth:

truth you have made known to us in the one

who is the truth,

our Savior Jesus Christ.  Amen.

*After Metropolitan Philaret of Moscow, 1867*

✠

# Wisdom of the Saints

*The writings and sayings of the men and women who have gone before us in the Communion of Saints can give us insight and encouragement as we seek to respond to the gospel and live our baptismal union with Christ for the sake of the world in our own day. Here are several passages which have to do with the heart. In scripture and tradition, the heart is understood as the core and center of what it means to be human. The disposition of our heart represents our fundamental orientation toward life and the One who gives life in all its fullness.*

*According to the Desert Fathers and Mothers of the fourth century, their essential work, achieved through a life of prayer and fasting and solitude, was the acquisition of a heart.*

*"Acquire a heart and you shall be saved" is one of their sayings that has come down to us across the centuries.*

*And what kind of a heart were they talking about? St. Isaac of Syria, writing in the seventh century, answers the question: it is a merciful heart. He then asks: What is a merciful heart? He then gives this answer:*

"It is a heart that burns with love for the whole of creation — for men and women, for the birds, for the beasts, for the demons, for every creature. When a person with a heart such as this thinks of the creatures or looks at them, his eyes are filled with tears. An overwhelming compassion makes his heart grow small and weak, and he cannot endure to hear or see any suffering, even the smallest pain, inflicted upon any creature. Therefore he never ceases to pray, with tears, even for the irrational animals, for the enemies of truth, and for those who do him evil, asking that they may be guarded and receive God's mercy. And for the reptiles also he prays with a great compassion, which rises up endlessly in his heart until he shines again and is glorious like God."

*The merciful heart described by St. Isaac is cosmic in its embrace: nothing is excluded but all is reconciled and healed through love, a love poured into our hearts by the Holy Spirit, a love which is nothing less than Christ's deathless love at work in us.*

*Thomas Merton has this to say about the heart:*

"If I allow Christ to use my heart in order to love my brothers and sisters with it, I will soon find that Christ, loving in me and through me, has brought to light Christ in my brothers and sisters. And I will find that the love of Christ in my brothers and sisters, loving me in return, has brought forth the image and reality of Christ in my own soul."

✠

*Reading these texts from the seventh century and from our own day invites us to pray for the gift of a heart full of mercy and compassion.*

Merciful God,
pour your love into my heart
    and make it one with the heart of Christ.
May Christ's compassion find a home in me
    and through me bring hope and healing to others.
    Amen.

✠ ✠ ✠ ✠ ✠

# VI

# My Soul is Athirst for God

## Approaching the Mystery

It is part of our human nature that since the beginning of time we, God's creatures, have used every means at hand in our efforts to approach, to ponder, to comprehend – even in the smallest measure – the ineffable mystery of God. We are told in the First Letter of John that we love because God "first loved us." Or, as St. Augustine of Hippo tells us, we seek God because God has first found us. However we may name divine Mystery, God has planted the yearning toward the divine within us.

In the midst of humanity's yearnings, the Word became flesh and dwelt among us. As a result of the Incarnation, whereby God's Eternal Word "through whom all things were made" took on our humanity in the person of Jesus, the physical and tangible have been imbued with the capacity to point to and manifest the divine. In virtue of the Incarnation we know that the visible and the concrete can serve to reveal dimensions of the divine Mystery.

☩

"Come, let us bow down, and bend the knee, and kneel before the Lord our Maker."

In addition to approaching divine Mystery through our senses, our bodies can be regarded as vehicles of our prayer. "Glorify God in your body," St. Paul tells us in the First Letter to the Corinthians. Prayer is not simply a matter of words or thoughts: the Holy Spirit who teaches us to pray also indwells our bodies. Classical disciplines such as fasting and abstinence, which are prescribed in the course of the Church Year, are ways of drawing our bodies into our prayer.

☩

*Since ancient times, various gestures and postures have supported and sustained Christians in their encounter with the divine. Kneeling and standing, raising our hands, bowing, bending the knee, and making the sign of the cross are traditional and hallowed ways of praying with our bodies. For example, as an aid to recollection on entering a church, it is customary to bow to the altar, which stands as the symbol of Christ's presence. The Reserved Sacrament, another sign of Christ's presence, may be acknowledged either with a profound bow or a bending of the knee. It is customary also to bow at ascriptions of praise to the Holy Trinity:*

Glory to the Father, and to the Son, and to the Holy Spirit: as it was in the beginning, is now, and will be for ever.  Amen.

Praise to the Holy and undivided Trinity, one God: as it was in the beginning, is now, and will be for ever. Amen.

✠

When we are baptized we are marked with the sign of the cross, and declared "Christ's own forever." Thereafter, when we trace the sign of the cross upon ourselves – from head to chest and from left to right shoulder – we remind ourselves that we are "not our own" but have been "bought with a price" through the life-giving death of Jesus upon the cross. This gesture is a recognition that through baptism we have been made limbs of Christ's risen body and thereby ministers of his reconciling love. The sign of the cross also serves in the manner of a punctuation mark at the beginning of or during prayer, or to emphasize particular moments in the liturgy, such as when receiving absolution or blessing.

To kneel in penitence, to raise our hands in prayer, to bow as we acclaim the mystery of the Trinity, to bend the knee in the presence of the Blessed Sacrament, or to mark ourselves with the sign of Christ's cross are all ways in which our bodies become an outward expression of an interior response to the mystery of God.

☩

For God alone my soul in silence waits.

*Psalm 62*

*There is an old Quaker aphorism: silence sorts and sifts us. Indeed, silence can be its own form of language. When we give ourselves over to silence and set aside the noise of the world in which we live and move and have our being, the Spirit can often speak with a "still small voice" that we would be unable to hear in the midst of our distractions and preoccupations. For many of us silence is perceived as an absence when, in fact, it can be experienced as a fullness, a fullness we can only know by allowing silence to sort and sift us. Sometimes the Spirit who prays within us is inviting us to go beyond thoughts and words and simply be still, embraced by the silent word. George Herbert describes prayer as God's breath in us returning to its birth.*

☩

*Paying attention to the rhythm of our breathing can help us to gather our mental and physical energies in order to wait in silence before God. At times of prayer or meditation, mindful breathing can help bring body and spirit together in a stance of availability to the Spirit.*

*Mindful breathing, sometimes in conjunction with other exercises such as certain forms of yoga, can become a form of prayer. With each breath we take in life itself: God's gift to us. And, with every exhalation we acknowledge and respond to that gift. Slow and rhythmic breathing joined to the recitation of a word or phrase from scripture, or perhaps the Jesus Prayer, can open the way for the Divine to encounter us freely in the secret place of our hearts.*

# Images of the Invisible

*The First Letter of John speaks of Jesus Christ as the Word of life who is apprehended by our senses: "What was from the beginning, what we have heard, what we have seen with our own eyes, what we have looked at and touched with our hands, concerning the word of life. . .we declare to you." What comes to us through our bodies and is apprehended by our five senses can help us to perceive and encounter the Divine: things of this earth and the fruit of human imagination and creativity can speak a revelatory word. We can find ourselves addressed by a mountain sunrise, a piece of music, an icon, a statue or other work of art, such as stained glass windows in a medieval cathedral, a cloud of fragrant incense, a flickering candle, a compassionate glance, the touch of a hand.*

*In the Eastern Christian tradition icons play a prominent role and are considered a pictorial form of scripture, depicting the mystery of Christ, the mystery of the church, and the revelation of Christ in the lives of the saints. The icon's highly stylized form is not meant to be realistic, but rather is to point to the spiritual and theological significance of the persons or events being represented. Because they are regarded as a form of scripture, icons are spoken of as being "written" rather than "painted," and the writing of icons is considered a gift given by the Spirit.*

*Increasingly icons have found their way into Western churches, as well as the homes of individual Christians. Centering our attention upon an icon, and letting it address us on its own terms, can help focus our prayer and be an opening to the mystery of God revealed in the life and death of Jesus and all that flows from his resurrection.*

*The following reflections upon the eight icons found in the color section of this book and on the cover are offered to you as invitations to prayer with suggestions of how each might be approached. As you contemplate them, pray that you may be led beyond what is represented to an encounter with the "mystery that has been hidden throughout the ages . . .which is Christ in you, the hope of glory."*

*(Colossians 1:26-27)*

# The Holy Trinity

*The icon of the Trinity draws upon the eighteenth chapter of the Book of Genesis in which we are told, "The Lord appeared to Abraham by the Oaks of Mamre. . .he looked up and saw three men standing near him." The appearance of God in the form of three men or angels has been interpreted as the revelation of God's interior life in the Persons of the Father, the Son, and the Holy Spirit. Abraham prepared food for his angelic visitors who ate under the oak depicted in the background.*

*As we contemplate the icon, we find ourselves standing in front of an altar table upon which stands a chalice symbolizing Jesus' self-gift in the eucharist. Christ sits in the center and the angels representing the Father and the Holy Spirit sit to his right and left. The inclination of their heads underscores the unity of their life and action animated by an eternal communion of love. This unending flow of love between the Persons of the Trinity has been likened to a circle dance into which we are drawn by the Holy Spirit in baptism. The eucharist then sustains and matures the life of the Trinity within us.*

*Our presence before the altar completes the circle, making us one with the Father, the Son, and the Holy Spirit.*

# The Annunciation

*The icon of the Annunciation draws from the Gospel of Luke (1:26-38) and depicts the encounter between Mary and the angel Gabriel. The angel's wide stance emphasizes the urgency of his mission, which is to announce God's choice of Mary to bear the "Son of the Most High."*

*According to tradition and the Infancy Gospel of James, Mary was spinning a purple thread when Gabriel greeted her. In the midst of her everyday life with its tasks and responsibilities, Mary receives God's call. She drops her spindle and raises her hand in perplexity and confusion. At the same time Gabriel extends his hand to impart his message. In response to Mary's wonderment, "How can this be?" the angel replies, "The Holy Spirit will come upon you and the power of the Most High will overshadow you."*

*In acknowledgment that what is passing between them is of God, both Mary and Gabriel are gazing upward toward rays descending from heaven.*

In the unfolding of our own lives, often when we least expect it, an invitation is extended that throws us into confusion. With Mary we find ourselves exclaiming, "How can this be?" And yet, if we are able to stammer as Mary did, "Let it be to me according to your word," and trust that the Holy Spirit will overshadow us and lead us forward, God's desire, God's word, will find fulfillment in us.

# The Virgin of Vladimir

*The icon of Mary with the infant Jesus is known as the Vladimir Mother of God or Our Lady of Loving-kindness. It is both a proclamation of the mystery of the Word made flesh and of the deep bond of love between Mary and her Son. The divine and the human dimensions of the Incarnation are set forth as one. With one hand Mary holds her Son and with the other she is inviting us to contemplate the mystery.*

*In a gesture of reciprocal loving-kindness Jesus, in the fullness of his humanity, embraces his mother. At the same time, his royal robe prefigures his "kingship" revealed on the cross.*

*Mary's solemn gaze focused upon her Son is suffused by the prophecy of Simeon uttered when she and Joseph presented Jesus in the Temple: "This child is destined for the falling and rising of many in Israel, and to be a sign that will be opposed so that the inner thoughts of many will be revealed – and a sword will pierce your own soul too" (Luke 2:34-35).*

*The Incarnation as presented to us in this icon is filled with tenderness devoid of sentimentality: the cost to both Mother and Son is present from the moment of Jesus' birth. Bearing the Word in our own lives is costly as well.*

## The Baptism of Christ

*The icon of Jesus' baptism, an event recorded in the gospels, is an invitation to reflect upon both Jesus' baptism and our own. According to the Gospel of Mark (1:9-11) as Jesus, having been baptized by John, was coming up out of the waters of the Jordan river, "he saw the heavens torn apart and the Spirit descending like a dove on him. And a voice came from heaven, 'You are my Son, the Beloved; with you I am well pleased.'"*

*The open space at the top of the icon indicates an opening of the heavens from which the Spirit, in the form of a dove, descends upon Jesus' head. In this way, the icon bears witness to the mystery of the Trinity: the communion of the Holy Spirit unites the Father and the Son in a relationship of love. Jesus' ministry begins at the Jordan not with an agenda imposed from on high, but with an overwhelming awareness of his belovedness. This awareness animates his preaching and teaching and makes it possible for him to address God with intimate affection as "Abba, Father."*

*Our baptism, before all else, is the declaration that we too are God's beloved sons and daughters. Our life then is a response: a living out of our being deeply loved.*

The nakedness of Jesus bears witness to the fact that "though he was in the form of God" he "emptied himself, taking the form of a slave, being born in human likeness. And being found in human form, he humbled himself and became obedient to the point of death – even death on a cross" (Philippians 2:6-8). Jesus stands in the water as though in a cave, signifying his burial and the fact that in baptism we are buried with Christ in his death and raised to newness of life by the power of the resurrection.

## The Transfiguration

The Transfiguration of Jesus (Mark 9:2-8) occurs at a turning point in Jesus' ministry and prepares the way for the journey up to Jerusalem and to the cross. Jesus ascends the mountain accompanied by Peter, James, and John. Jesus' appearance is then altered: "He was transfigured before them, and his clothes became dazzling white, such as no one on earth could bleach them. And there appeared to them Elijah and Moses, who were talking with Jesus."

Elijah and Moses on Jesus' right and left represent the Prophets and the Law bearing witness to Christ. Again, as at Jesus' baptism, a voice from heaven is heard: "This is my

Son, the Beloved; listen to him." The three rays emanating from Jesus' radiance indicate that this is a moment of Trinitarian self-revelation. The three disciples fall back in fear and wonder, overwhelmed by the magnitude of the mystery that has overtaken them.

We too are surrounded by mystery: the world around us and all living things, in virtue of their creation, are luminous with God's glory. Our preoccupations and distractions blind us and keep us from seeing that this is so. Some commentators have observed that what changed on that mountaintop was not the person of Jesus but the perceptions of Peter, James, and John. They became "eyewitnesses of his majesty" because they were able to see their Master as he truly was. The three disciples saw in Jesus the radiance that had always been his, a radiance of death-defying love that embraces and sustains all that is. As you contemplate the icon of the Transfiguration, may you too be given the grace to see.

## The Crucifixion

*The icon of the Crucifixion brings to mind a prayer that begins, "Lord Jesus Christ, you stretched out your arms of love on the hard wood of the cross that everyone might come within the reach of your saving embrace." Jesus' extended arms embrace those who stand below the cross: Mary and an accompanying woman on the left, and John and the centurion on the right.*

*Behind the cross are the walls of Jerusalem and below the cross is a skull, the skull of Adam. Through a fissure in the rock, the blood of Jesus, the Second Adam according to St. Paul, brings redemption to the first Adam who represents humankind.*

*The cross, therefore, is set before us not only as an instrument of death, but as the source of life. Mary and John extend their hands and invite us to contemplate the mystery. "But now in Christ Jesus you who were once far off have been brought near by the blood of Christ" (Ephesians 2:13).*

*The acclamation from the Good Friday liturgy could be part of your prayer before this icon: We glory in your cross, O Lord, and praise and glorify your holy resurrection; for by virtue of your cross joy has come to the whole world."*

## The Descent into Hell

*The icon of the Descent into Hell proclaims the mystery of the resurrection. Its scriptural foundation is found in the First Letter of Peter, in which we are told that the risen Christ "went and made a proclamation to the spirits in prison, who in former times did not obey. . . ." The traditional form of the Apostles' Creed is more specific: "He descended into hell."*

*Christ, standing on the broken-down doors of Hell, grasps Adam by the wrist, and Eve as well in some depictions. In many depictions, in the black abyss below Christ's feet are locks and chains and other signs of bondage. Christ is pulling, indeed yanking Adam, who stands for us all, out of the constricting space of his tomb into the force field of new and unbounded resurrection life.*

*In the words of an ancient Easter homily, the risen One declares to Adam and Eve, and to us: "Out of love for you and your descendants I now by my authority command all who are held in bondage to come forth, all who are in darkness to be enlightened, all who are sleeping to arise. I order you, O sleeper, to awake. I did not create you to be held a prisoner in hell. Rise from the dead, for I am the life of the* dead. Rise up, work of my hands, you who were created in my image. Rise, let us leave this place, for you are in me and I am in you; together we form only one person and we cannot be separated."

As you contemplate the icon, let Christ address you. Ask him to grasp you by the wrist and pull you forcibly into freedom and out of the various forms of bondage that keep you from living into the fullness of who you are called to be "in grace and truth."

Resurrection is not always pleasant or easy; it can sometimes feel like death, as old patterns and old perceptions give way to the new. Perhaps Adam would have preferred the safety and security of his tomb, and did not altogether welcome the firm grasp of the One who declared, "I am the resurrection and the life."

Encounters with resurrection oblige us to acknowledge and hand over our fears and resistance. "Do not by hanging down break from the hand / Which, as it riseth, raiseth thee," urges George Herbert in a poem entitled "The Dawning."

## Christic the Savior

*Remembering that icons are a form of pictorial scripture, let the icon speak to you. Let the eyes of Christ look into your eyes and search the depths of your heart. Let Jesus, who fully shared our humanity, and knows you better than you know yourself, meet you with his calm and steady gaze. Let the Spirit of Christ bring to your awareness whatever Christ, in the wideness of his mercy, wishes you to know about him and about you and about your relationship with each other. As you contemplate the icon, you might be moved to pray the Jesus Prayer, quietly and gently:* Lord Jesus Christ, Son of the living God, have mercy on me, a sinner.

# Guardian Angel

*The icon on the cover of this book invites us to reflect upon the ministry of angels. The word "angel" means "messenger." As such, angels appear frequently in the pages of Holy Scripture, where they serve to indicate the immediacy of God's presence and the urgency of God's word. At times angels are identified as God, as in the case of the angels who visit Abraham at the Oaks of Mamre, as we see in the icon of the Trinity.*

*In Western Christianity there is a notion of guardian angels: that is, particular angels assigned to each of us as special friends and messengers from God whose purpose, in the words of the liturgy, is to "help and defend us here on earth." The wings of angels as depicted in various forms of art, rather than an actual physical attribute, are symbolic of their function, which is to convey God's loving care and purpose from the heights of God's mystery to the depths of the human heart.*

Angels can take human form and speak to us in the voices of those around us, those close to us, and strangers we meet along the way. As you contemplate the icon of the Guardian Angel, ask the Holy Spirit to bring to your awareness those who have served as special messengers of God's loving care and purpose in your life. Allow yourself to stand ready for further encounters with God's special helpers. As well, be open to the possibility that God will ask you in the days ahead to be a messenger to others of his loving care.

✠ ✠ ✠ ✠ ✠

# Afterword

*God's grace, as I hope this book has made clear, is developmental over time. As much as we might wish that spiritual insight and maturity came quickly, we must be slowly shaped and formed by the unerring, and often inscrutable, tugs and pulls of the Holy Spirit who knows us more fully than we know ourselves. On our part, this calls for patient trust before God, a trust wonderfully described in the following words from the Jesuit priest and scientist, Pierre Teilhard de Chardin.*

## Patient Trust

Above all, trust in the slow work of God.

We are quite naturally impatient in everything
    to reach the end without delay.

We should like to skip the intermediate stages.

We are impatient of being on the way to something
    unknown, something new.

And yet it is the law of all progress
     that it is made by passing through
     some stages of instability —
     and that it may take a very long time.

And so I think it is with you.
     Your ideas mature gradually — let them grow,
     let them shape themselves, without undue haste.
Don't try to force them on,
     as though you could be today what time
     (that is to say grace and circumstances
     acting on your own good will)
     will make of you tomorrow.

Only God can say what this new spirit
     gradually forming within you will be.
Give our Lord the benefit of believing
     that his hand is leading you,
and accept the anxiety of feeling yourself
     in suspense and incomplete.

*Offered in the pages of this book are various ways in which men and women across the centuries have made room for encounters with "the grace of our Lord Jesus Christ, and the love of God, and the communion of the Holy Spirit." (2 Corinthians 13:14) If in some small way they help you to open yourself to that encounter they will have served their purpose.*

## Source Notes

Prayers from *A New Zealand Prayer Book* are used by permission of the General Secretary of the Province of the Anglican Church in Aotearoa, New Zealand and Polynesia.

Unless otherwise noted, all other prayers are taken or adapted from the 1979 Book of Common Prayer or *Enriching Our Worship 1*, or are of the author's own composition.

"Patient Trust" by Pierre Teilhard de Chardin from *Hearts on Fire: Praying with Jesuits*, Institute of Jesuit Sources, 1993.

"Word" by Madeleine L'Engle from *The Weather of the Heart: Poems*, 1973. H. Shaw, Wheaton, IL. Used by permission.

The icons of the Guardian Angel (cover), the Virgin of Vladimir, and Christ the Savior © Peter Pearson. Used by permission.

The icon of the Annunciation © Kathryn Carrington. Used by permission.

The following icons are from Art Resource, New York, used by permission: the Holy Trinity, Andrei Rublev, c. 1410, Tretyakov Gallery, Moscow: the Baptism of Christ, Anonymous, 14th century, National Museum, Belgrade, Serbia; the Transfiguration, Theopan the Greek, c. 1403, Tretyakov Gallery, Moscow; the Crucifixion, School of Novgorod, 17th century, the Louvre, Paris; the Descent into Hell, Anonymous, 15th century, Tretyakov Gallery, Moscow.